In *Human Doing & Human Being* Costa addresses both psychological and spiritual aspects of personal development. He holds your hand every step of the way through self-development exercises and audio sessions to help you find or rediscover your sense of worth — your "worth-full-ness". He then invites you to open your heart and mind to discover more about your true purpose as he guides you to experience your divine nature.

A powerful, timely contribution to personal development.

— Dame Irene Loudon DGSJ, MRSPH,
theologian, hypnotherapist, psychotherapist,
counsellor and personal development coach

# HUMAN *DOING* & HUMAN *BEING*

## THE EVOLUTIONARY SELF-HELP GUIDE TO ACHIEVING YOUR LIFE'S OUTER & INNER PURPOSE NOW

## Costa Lambrias
### The UK'S Self-Esteem Doctor

~ an *Answers Within* book ~
Manchester UK 2014

**Human Doing & Human Being – The Evolutionary Self-Help Guide To Achieving Your Life's Outer & Inner Purpose NOW**
**Published by Answers Within**
© **Costa Lambrias, 2014**

Copyrights & Permissions

"This Be The Verse" from The Complete Poems Of Philip Larkin by Philip Larkin, edited by Archie Burnett. Copyright © 2012 by The Estate of Philip Larkin. Reprinted by permission of Farrar, Straus and Giroux, LLC and Faber & Faber Ltd.

Sweet Dreams (Are Made Of This). Words & Music by Annie Lennox & Dave Stewart © Copyright 1983 BMG Music Publishing Limited and Universal Music Publishing MGB Ltd. All rights in the World excluding the U.S. and Canada Administered by Universal Music Publishing MGB Limited. All Rights in the U.S. and Canada Administered by Universal Music — MGB Songs. All Rights Reserved. International Copyright Secured. Reprinted by permission of Hal Leonard Corporation and Music Sales Limited.

ISBN: 978-0-9927491-0-1

This Guide is dedicated to Panayiotis (Takis) Lambrias and Chrystalleni Christodoulou, Ameer Jahan and Madihah Noor, and to my brothers and sisters, present and future. My most sincere wish is that it assists you on your journey to abundance and fulfilment.

# CONTENTS

## Part Two: Human Being

# FOREWORD

The older I get, the more excited I get about the future and what lies in store for us. Along with all the new scientific discoveries, there is the prospect of new writers and thinkers coming to the fore. Ideas and theories that once would have been considered outlandish and not to be taken seriously are now being not only published, but utilised, taken further, and explored with a view to them being accepted by Science.

I look along my book shelves (there are 5000 books in this small house) and the thought that is uppermost in my mind is "If only I had had these books when I was training with the Inner Light School in the sixties."

The book you now hold in your hands is among those treasured books. When I first read it, my thoughts were "How different things were in my young days." A book like this would have been such a Godsend. It would have reassured me that I was not alone in the way my mind worked.

It has been written with insight and dedication, and is filled with knowledge that has been won through dedication and hard work. All too often, books are written simply by reading someone else's work and embroidering what has already been said. Here you have original work based on the *personal* work and *personal* experience of the author — the highest accolade that can be given to any work.

I recommend it to my students and Supervisors in the Servants of the Light School.

— Dolores Ashcroft-Nowicki
Director of Studies for SOL

# PREFACE

*This Guide and "Owner's Manual" is for **you***! *It has everything to do with your quality of life as a human being and your birthright to be happy. It empowers you to approach life with a greater belief in yourself and to live your life with true purpose. It will enable you to squeeze twice as much fulfilment and joy from each and every moment.*

There is a two-fold purpose behind this book. Its aim in Part One **Human Doing** is to undo all the negative unconscious programming that has so far prevented you from living life to the full and making a success of every area of your life in this world: relationships, careers and lifestyle aspirations. Since 1990 I have helped thousands of people to overcome lowly self-perceptions and to increase their levels of self-esteem so that they could now feel worthy of receiving all of Life's riches. Once I realized that the powerful transformational processes I use could be expressed through the medium of the written word and via the internet, the idea of this book came into being. I have taught my self-development processes to other therapists around the world, and now is the perfect time to share them directly with you.

The aim of Part Two **Human Being** is to answer the fundamental questions about the purpose of human existence. I promise that if you approach Part Two with an open mind and an open heart, you will receive far more spiritual riches than you could possibly imagine. I am not talking about following a religion, but instead enjoying your own personal practical and direct experience of the Love that breathes you, the universe and all of creation. Please approach this part of your Guide as an opportunity to grow in consciousness and spiritual awareness, and to fulfil the inner purpose to your life.

This book has taken six years to write. The self-development processes, which I include in downloadable audio form, have been used one-to-one with clients for over twenty-three years, but their genesis began over forty years ago when I was searching for answers to the questions *"Who/What am I? Why am I here?"* The fulfilment I received as a result of this quest has led to my two greatest passions in life, apart from my passion for Life itself — they are about improving quality of life for others, and Consciousness. Fortunately, I combine both in my *"therapy with consciousness!"*

I had been a "Seeker" from an early age, searching for an experience that I had come from before birth and would be returning to at death, but needed to reconnect with during this lifetime in order to provide purpose, meaning and fulfilment to my existence. As a child, I always had the feeling that I was "different". Even though I was the eldest of two sets of twins, I had the feeling of "not belonging". Despite being loved by my parents and siblings, I always thought of myself as the "black sheep" of the family. I was different but didn't know why.

I had a very enquiring mind and asked questions about everything because I wanted to know more. I remember a phase around the age of twelve of being completely fascinated by the mystery of life and death. I would use an empty glass container to catch large flies in the store room of my father's shop and then hide them in a corner of the freezer. Several hours later when they were "dead", I would retrieve them and place them outside in the sunlight. Within minutes they would thaw out and fly away. This raised more questions than answers!

Soon after this period I was taken seriously ill with pleurisy and was confined to bed for several weeks. This led to my own "Francis of Assisi" experience. Without my concerned mother knowing, I would stumble out of my sickbed and quietly unlock the door to my bedroom balcony in order to commune with the birds. In my feeble condition and altered state of awareness, I posed no threat to these tiny creatures and they would come and visit my balcony and sing to me while I did my best to continue our heartfelt conversations by mimicking their sounds.

As a teenager I recall going to the local library in order to study for some school exams. I was amazed, thrilled and nervously excited to discover a book there called "The Meaning of Life". At long last, someone was going to answer my questions! I read that book in a single day. I remember reading it up to the final chapter and the answer hadn't been revealed yet. I concentrated hard until I reached the last two pages of the book. Reading with even more intensity than before,

I slowly digested the final sentences that would explain the very purpose to my existence... and I was left no wiser than before!

A few years later, in my first year of university, I was going through an identity crisis. I'd become an atheist because I couldn't understand why there was so much injustice in the world and how a God, if one existed, could allow innocent babies to die. For over a year I walked around Exeter University with *Who/What am I?* etched vividly in blue ink on the upper left leg of my jeans. Surely in this so-called "bastion of learning" I would find one tutor, professor or student of theology who knew the answer to that question?

It was during this time, as a student of French language and literature, that I had my own personal experience of what French Existential author and philosopher Jean-Paul Sartre called "la Nausée" (Nausea). Ironically, it happened to me while I was delivering a literature assignment to my French tutor. I knocked on her office door. There was no reply, so I prepared to place my papers in the box on the wall next to her door. As I was doing so, I noticed that my tutor's name had been typed onto a strip of white paper which was Scotch taped to the glass front of her box. The right-hand edge of the tape had come unstuck and had curled up. It was dirty and discoloured with the specks of dust and dirt that had accumulated over time on its sticky surface. This was in marked contrast to the rest of the stuck down Scotch tape which was clear and clean. On seeing this grubby symbol of impermanence and decay, I immediately felt sick to the pit of my stomach. I was overwhelmed in my head and in my gut by a sense of absolute futility and transience, an overpowering feeling of the meaningless of human existence: a tiny and insignificant speck of dust (me), a passenger on another insignificant speck of dust (Earth) in the vastness of Space and Time — that *you're here, then you're gone — so what's the point of it all?!* This insight into the human condition was to repeat itself very strongly a few months later, over a year after I had worn my heart on my sleeve (or rather on my jeans with *"Who/What am I?"*) and throughout which time not one of the University's professors, dons, tutors, academics or students of theology had answered my question about the meaning of existence.

It was December 1973. I was sat in my room in one of the university halls of residence. I could see through my window other students going home for the Christmas vacation while I was still here with an assignment to finish. I asked myself "Why am I doing this essay?" The answer came: *To get a degree.* "Why do I want a degree?" *To get a good job.* "Why do I want a good job?" *To get a car, a house, a family.* "And then what?" The answer to that question presented itself to me as the image of a dark railway tunnel with a big train heading straight for me: *Death!* "Well there has to be more to Life than just that! If that's all that Life's about, then what's the point of living? I might as well not be here." (Killing myself seemed the logical conclusion, one I hadn't considered seriously before.) *NO! IF YOU KILL YOURSELF YOU WON'T GET THE ANSWER!* That "voice" was very strong! Just then there was a knock on my door, and it was only months later when I was fully immersed in my spiritual lifestyle (as described in Part Two of this book) that I realized that the person at my door had been directed to me at the perfect time to guide me to the experience that answered all my questions.

Having received the answer to my spiritual questions, I chose to live a renunciate lifestyle which included meditating two to four hours every day on this wonderful internal reality, all the while feeling more and more "detached" from worldly reality despite working in a nine-to-five job. When my lifestyle changed, and I returned to the world and eventually became a hypnotherapist, I found that my spiritual experiences had given me an understanding of how human beings "work" that was more insightful and useful than the hypnotherapy model of conscious and unconscious/subconscious mind. I practised, and still do, what I call "therapy with consciousness!" Also, as I was still meditating regularly on the supreme consciousness within, I was "getting" information that was invaluable in forming new processes of therapy to help my clients with their damaged childhood and chronic low self-esteem issues.

Today, as the UK's Self-Esteem Doctor®, teaching my inner child therapy and Soul Concern workshops around the world, I sincerely believe that there are two hidden and ignored factors contributing to the disenchantment of modern society. The first is what I call *the hidden disease affecting the quality of life of most members of modern society*, presented to me day after day by client after client: the completely curable affliction of low self-esteem.

Classic symptoms of low self-esteem can present as low aspirations in life (avoiding challenges or promotions), and forming unequal or unfulfilling personal relationships, because the sufferer does not believe he or she deserves any better. Even those who have succeeded in the world can feel "a fraud" and unworthy of any achievements. There are many people who have already tried positive affirmations, the Secret, the Law of Attraction and Cosmic Ordering, who are still waiting for positive changes to manifest in their life. This is because no matter how hard you try in life, if the underlying belief in your psyche is that of "I am not worthy" then this is what needs to change first! *Part One of this book is all about making the deep and positive changes that will enable you to change for the better what you receive in life.*

The second factor contributing to the disenchantment of modern society is one that I am witnessing more regularly, especially in some clients presenting with symptoms of depression. Its symptoms also include despair, hopelessness, that there doesn't seem to be a point to their existence. This is entirely due to a lack of spirituality and the ignorance of one's true essence, which religion alone cannot fulfil. Part Two of this book addresses these issues.

Writing Part Two, **Human Being**, over the last two years has resulted in a greater focus on my own spiritual connection in order to maintain the inspiration required for inspiration itself to manifest on the page — there are many "quotes" in Part Two that allegedly came through me that still surprise me with their insight. This part of my journey has also enabled me to realize a long-held ambition of mine to lead workshops on Consciousness that impact powerfully onto the personal, spiritual and professional aspects of people's lives. Love begets Gratitude… *Thank you!*

# ACKNOWLEDGMENTS

I want to thank all those people who may or may not know that they had a hand in this book: Vanessa Talbot, Wendy Millgate, Liz Rhodes, Robert Wilson, Christopher Lloyd Clarke, Joel Friedlander, Michele DeFilippo, Valerie Reay, Laurita Tomlinson-Smith, and a very special thanks to Coby Zvikler and Gillian Brown without whose support this book would never have been completed.

I wish to acknowledge the contribution of all my clients, teachers and guides, past, present and future, and to Eckhart Tolle whose expressions of Truth inspired me to write *Human Being*. Divine inspiration and enlightenment are due to my teacher Prem who has guided me since 1973 and to my beloved M who literally turned my world outside in.

# INTRODUCTION

Whenever I am asked by clients *"What's the purpose of Life? Why am I here?"* I usually reply that that is the easy question! The answer is *"To be happy!"* The real question should be *"**How** to be happy?"* I recommend you take advantage of all the self-improvement sessions outlined in Part One before benefiting from the insights, truths and revelations of Part Two about the inner life that has eluded so many human beings so far. Because these two Parts are about different worlds and realities (one outer, the other inner), my language and writing style in each part reflects this. One will appeal to your logical mind and imagination, the other to your heart, your true soul essence.

Part One **Human Doing** addresses your situation in the world where Security, Love, Success, Reward, Abundance and Prosperity are the goals. It explains how essential a healthy self-image is, and it introduces you to powerful inner resources we all have but rarely use. By using the audio self-development sessions that accompany this handbook to reverse unconscious childhood or environmental negative programming, you will find yourself enjoying within a matter of weeks unprecedented levels of confidence and self-esteem. So deep are the changes with these proven processes that you will deserve, attract and be able to enjoy "all the good things in life".

Part Two **Human Being** is all about you as a spiritual being. Have you ever felt that there has to be more to life? I hope so because it is in our very nature to ask that question! Reading **Human Being** will awaken further the seeker in you and inspire you to find the true peace and contentment that is always inside you and beyond a finite world which for most human beings offers only a fragile sense of fulfilment.

# Owner's Manual: *Hints & Tips*

*C*ongratulations on acquiring a human body! Whether this is your first or most recent incarnation, there are several "Hints & Tips" we recommend you follow in order to enjoy *maximum quantity and quality of life.*

## Care

### 1. Physical
Look after your body and it will look after you. Healthy food, water between meals, and a good standard of shelter and clothing are vital components to achieving a longer time span with your body.

### 2. Environmental
We cannot emphasize enough a commonsense approach. Avoid if at all possible taking your body into high-risk areas. Extreme climates and territories with a risk or actual threat of war or disease must be avoided.

### 3. *Good Mental Health*

Your emotional and psychological wellbeing is as important to the quality of life as good physical health. It is recommended that you *take the self-diagnostic test* in Part One immediately in order to ascertain which of the self-development sessions are the most suitable and beneficial for you. Thus the attainment and enjoyment of *your goals in this world are virtually guaranteed* as a result of the natural boosts to your personal levels of self-esteem and self-worth.

### 4. *Good Spiritual Health (NEW for 2014!)*

In response to a growing number of our valued customers who questioned the very purpose of owning a human body, we have decided the time is now right to provide invaluable information in Part Two about *your true self.* We trust that the provision of this essential information will assist in *answering all your present and future questions about Life,* and will lead you to fulfil in this current incarnation your potential for inner peace, love, unshakeable security and a zest for living.

We strongly recommend that you read Part One before Part Two in order to maximize the benefits and gains achievable from this Owner's Manual.

We trust you are now ready to discover that **all the answers are within…** *Happy Living!*

# PART ONE

# *Human Doing*

# CHAPTER ONE
## *The Key to Enjoying Life*

> *"The quality of your life is not to be measured by what possessions, status or lifestyle you have or don't have, but rather by how you feel about yourself."*
> (Costa Lambrias, Self-Esteem Doctor)

ife. Some would say the most precious gift. But now that you have life, how do you get the most out of it? Chances are good, if you are reading this book, that you live in a so-called civilized society and already enjoy a reasonable quality of life when compared to human beings living in parts of the world where food, clothing or shelter may be in short supply; or where there is a threat to life from war or disease. Assuming also that you enjoy a reasonable level of good health, I ask you to consider this: that *the quality of your life, and your enjoyment of everything you have in your life, is governed by your level of self-esteem.*

It doesn't matter if you desire — or already have — wealth, fame, a great lifestyle, material possessions, status or position; if your self-esteem is not good then you will always find it difficult to enjoy what you have. First of all, a lack of self-worth could be preventing you from attracting "all the good things in life" which you believe would make your life better; and secondly, if you do manage to attain any of these, the same condition prevents you from truly enjoying them anyway! Society, parents and peers may have programmed you with their expectations for you to feel inadequate unless you have a great job, income and lifestyle; so much so that these oftentimes unspoken expectations and pressures on you have now become identified by you as your own goals and desires. Nevertheless, if your childhood lacked consistent love and support, nurturing and encouragement, validation and affection from parents or carers, then the biggest program running in your psyche will be one of *"I'm not worthy, I don't deserve."*

Since 1990 I have met with many clients in my private hypnotherapy practice who, on the face of it, would appear to have all that they wanted. Yet time after time, many would tell me that they felt "a fraud", unworthy of what they have. This includes those who in actuality do perform confidently in their work environment. Some of them in very senior management or directorship level positions expect to be "found out" by the CEO, despite being complimented on how well they are performing and how much of an asset to the company they are. That's because one of the symptoms of chronic low self-esteem is that compliments enter one ear to exit immediately out of the other! As I will explain later, it is not unusual for some low self-esteemers to be high achievers, but just like the majority of sufferers who prefer to avoid most challenges that come their way, the underlying feelings of worthlessness that usually originate in early childhood days run very deep! They are as deeply ingrained in their psyche as are the birth names they were given, and with which they so strongly identify for the rest of their life.

Thankfully, with the tried and tested powerful and effective processes included with this book, positive changes in your personality, outlook, attitude and quality of life can occur for you just as easily as it has for the thousands of clients who have sought my assistance one-to-one. The first step is to take the Self-Esteem Test in Chapter Two.

For those of you fortunate enough to already enjoy great levels of self-esteem, I recommend that you listen to the specific self-development sessions that the self-esteem test advises are best suited to you. Doing so will assist you to maintain your positive and optimistic attitude and your winning mentality, and will keep you motivated to attract into your life even more abundance and gifts for you to enjoy. The Universe has an infinite amount of gifts to bestow on those who recognize that they are special (we all are!) and are ready to receive. So, why not you?

# CHAPTER TWO

# Step One: Self-Diagnosis

Self-Esteem is defined in many dictionaries as "confidence in one's own worth or abilities" and as "a good opinion of oneself; self-confidence". With over twenty years' experience as the Self-Esteem Doctor®, I believe there is more to say about the difference between low and good self-esteem. For the many clients I have seen suffering with low self-esteem there is a consistent symptom of *"not feeling as good as other people... feeling unworthy..."* even *"worthlessness"*. They come to see me to feel *"as good as"*, but for me "worthy" and "worthiness" doesn't quite cut it to describe good self-esteem. It's more than that, it's "worthfullness": full of worth, brimming with the potential to achieve; deserving, and able to accept, the best in life.

Your first step to worth-fullness is to take the Self-Esteem Test and discover which of the included self-development sessions will most benefit you. There are two self-esteem diagnostics: #1 is "Easy-Peasy" (EZPZ), #2 requires you to think more. Why not take both?

## *The EZPZ Self-Esteem Test #1*
The guide time for completion is two to three minutes.

*1. Measuring Your Confidence*
Thinking about your confidence levels, would you say

> *A*: You only lack confidence in one or two specific situations, e.g. because of a phobia or whenever you're the focus of attention. Do you get anxious or nervous in formal, group or social situations?

> OR *B*: You have never lacked confidence in any situation, and you can't imagine any situation where you would.

> OR *C*: Your lack of confidence extends to most areas of your life, in other words it's a *general* rather than *specific* lack of confidence, and you have a tendency to compare yourself unfavourably to others.

*2. Time Scale*
Assuming *1C* above applies, is your general lack of confidence

> *A*: A recent development only, due to circumstances beyond your control, and in contrast to how you used to feel for the greater part of your life?

> OR *B*: A feature of your life since adulthood?

> OR *C*: Something you have always had, even in childhood?

## 3. Childhood

It is important to take your time to seriously consider your answer to the following questions.

Which one of A, B, C or D best describes your childhood?

*A.* Genuinely happy.

*B.* Not so good.

*C.* Really very bad, i.e. "crap."

*D.* Can't remember.

## 4. Parenting

Throughout your childhood, were your parents or main carers physically demonstrably affectionate to you? In other words, apart from perhaps bedtime or when you were ill or hurt, did they regularly hold, kiss or cuddle you?

*A.* Mother or main female did.

OR *B.* Mother or main female did not, or was not around.

AND *C.* Father or main male did.

OR *D.* Father or main male did not, or was not around.

Now add up your scores to discover where you are on the self-esteem scale.

1A=1, 1B=0, 1C=2; 2A=1, 2B=2, 2C=3; 3A=0, 3B=2, 3C=4, 3D=3; 4A=0, 4B=3, 4C=0, 4D=2

*0–2*   Congratulations to you and your parents. A secure upbringing with positive and loving role models means the world is your oyster. Fine-tune yourself for success with Sessions 1, 4 and 5.

*3–7*   You sometimes feel vulnerable and lacking in self-assurance. Address any negative programs and symptoms with Sessions 1, 2, 4 and 5 so that you can attract and accept abundance and satisfaction in every area of your life.

*8–14*   Your low self-esteem affects most areas of your life, especially relationships. The Self-Esteem Doctor prescribes Sessions 1, 2, 3, 4 and 5 so that you can address childhood issues and become the happy and confident child and adult you deserve to be.

## *Self-Esteem Test #2*

This more comprehensive diagnostic tool is an essential part of the preparation for playing self-development session 3. If you scored less than 7 on the EZPZ Test above, you might still like to take it to double-check your rating on the self-esteem scale. You can find it in Chapter 6.

## The SIX *Answers Within* audio
## Self-Development sessions

## Human Doing

Session 1: *The Confidence Booster*
Play this first to get the whole of your mind, including your subconscious, on board straightaway with your new positive agenda. It will increase your sense of wellbeing in social and formal situations, and result in huge improvements in how confident and relaxed you are in all your interactions with others. Especially effective for when all eyes are on you.

Session 2: *The Multi-Level De-Stressor*
Extremely powerful, not just for protecting you from everyday stress but also for gaining release from emotional baggage, negative mood states, and a great many psychosomatic disorders and illnesses. Worth the price of the book on its own!

Session 3: *Meet and Heal your Inner Child*
Allows you to permanently reverse the effects of a damaged childhood — a gentle yet powerful transformational process. Gender-specific male and female inner child sessions are included.

Session 4: *The Supreme Performance and Self-Esteem Booster*
This session allows you to rewrite any negative programs, after which you'll be unstoppable and unshakeable — confident and self-assured in every situation and with any new challenge!

Session 5: *Your Goals*

Knocks out any remnants of self-doubt and focuses you on attaining success and happiness. You will literally make it happen!

## Human Being

Session 6: *A Glimpse*

This "trancey, trippy" session literally takes you out of yourself in order to provide you with insights into your inner self and into who and what you really are. It serves as a gentle introduction to your connection with your spiritual self and a new way of Being.

# CHAPTER THREE

## *The Secrets of the Mind: Reprogramming for Success*

For you to appreciate just how powerful the audio self-development sessions are, some understanding of how your mind works would be helpful. Nearly everybody is aware of their *conscious mind*, the part that does the thinking when we are awake. In fact some people believe this part is the real "me" inside the body. However, beneath the surface in exactly the same way as the biggest part of an iceberg is not visible to most of us, there is the *subconscious mind* which is far more powerful than the more obvious conscious mind. The subconscious automatically runs all your programs, including the ones you don't like or want. These can include phobias, addictions, and negative patterns of behaviour. The conscious mind has very little influence on the Subconscious; on the other hand, the subconscious, because of its programming, can affect positively or negatively everything about you: your physical health (immune system, illnesses), emotional and psychological states, attitudes of mind, vulnerabilities, and certainly your confidence levels and how you perform in each and every situation or challenge that comes your way in life.

The *Answers Within* audio self-development sessions have been specifically designed to engage your subconscious mind and bring about positive changes. Yes, your conscious mind will still be aware of what is being said as your body relaxes in line with the suggestions in each session; even so, your subconscious is taking on board the positive suggestions and begins to make those changes at the deepest level. Repetition is the key. Regular listening to each session allows the all-powerful subconscious to dump another load of negative programming as each positive suggestion is reinforced.

And beyond the mind, there is *soul* and *higher self.* I believe that when I am "in session" with a client then something happens at a "higher" level, not just at the subconscious level. If you and I are open to the positive changes that you seek, then my consciousness (in this context meaning "awareness of our true spiritual nature") and energy, as well as my therapist's voice and tone, together with the intent for your highest good, enable that to happen almost automatically. If we think of the icebergs analogy, it may appear that you and I are two separate entities supported in an ocean of water, but think again! Some of us actually recognize that in our true essence we are fundamentally one hundred percent water with no separation. If you can remind yourself of that truth whenever you listen to the sessions, then you improve your chances of success as you open up on every level to receiving positive change in your life.

On a practical level, it is important is to keep to the structure of the book and to play the self-development sessions in the correct order, after having done the relevant preparation first. In this way you maximize your chances of success. The publishers and I cannot take any responsibility if you do not keep to this recommended format. Within one to two months, if you have followed all the guidelines, you could be enjoying far greater levels of self-esteem and confidence in every area of your life.

If you are aware that you are suffering from severe psychological disorders, then you would be wise to take advantage of the support you would gain by having one-to-one sessions with a professional therapist rather than taking the risk of doing it all on your own. Check out the Resources section at the end of Part One for more details if you are not already in therapy.

Now we come to the exciting part of beginning to make powerful and positive changes in your confidence and self-esteem, and how you relate to the world around you! As your relationship with yourself changes and improves, so your expectations of Life increase, and your raised vibration and inner comfort with yourself resonate outward and begin the process of attracting to you all that you deserve. Please be sure to read all the Preparation notes before playing each recommended *Answers Within* session.

## CHAPTER FOUR

# *Boost Your Confidence*

Before playing the first of the *Answers Within* audio self-development sessions, it would be good to explain to you just how and why they work. There are two main criteria that guarantee success for virtually all my face-to-face clients which will also apply to you. First of all, you need to have a sincere desire for change — you do it for yourself and not because someone else has recommended it and you feel under pressure from that well-meaning person to try it out. Whether you believe this process is going to work for you or not, as long as there is a desire from you for something in your life to change for the better, then you are open to receive. Secondly, in order for the desired positive changes to plant themselves and take root at a sufficiently deep and effective level, all that is required in order to access your subconscious mind is a light degree of relaxation. That's right, you don't need to go "deep" or "under" (whatever that means!) or be "out of it". Through the careful use of specific words, and the pace and tone of my voice, as well as the use of music and

17

explicit suggestions of relaxation, your body should get to relax quite easily. And if your mind is no longer racing away with you, then I am confident that the "therapy" or transformative part of each *Answers Within* audio self-development session is going to be effective for you.

Each session will typically start with a physical relaxation induction which will lead into a nature scene to engage your mind and your imagination. This scene may form a necessary component of the therapy process that follows. I am fortunate to have been "guided" when composing some of these scenes — sometimes the significance of certain phrases or parts of a scene has only been realized several months after they came into my awareness. And so it will be for you: your logical, analytical left brain (the conscious mind, if you will) may "understand" everything and relax accordingly, and yet may fail to grasp the significance of metaphors, symbols and imagery that appeal to the creative, intuitive and imaginative right brain (which can be said to be representative of the subconscious).

To conclude, you are very much aware of what is going on around you when listening to the sessions. Even so, you are still able to enjoy a relaxed state which most people compare to daydreaming. I strongly recommend the use of headphones to minimize the noises and distractions in your environment.

## Preparation

As the *Confidence Booster* is the first session to be played, I will start with a very basic physical relaxation induction, asking you to tense and relax certain groups of muscles. You will need to make yourself comfortable first. If you have the use of a reclining chair and footstool, that is ideal and preferable to lying on a bed. Contrary to popular belief, you must not fall asleep! If you do fall asleep you may have gone too deep. There is a chance that your subconscious will now be enjoying a much deeper altered state than is required and be engaged in that dream world's reality, symbols and imagery. This would leave very little room for the subconscious to take on board any of the content of the session. This is why it is risky to play your sessions when you are tired and likely to fall asleep, so I ask you to please avoid lying on a bed if possible when starting out on this self-improvement program. If you wear glasses please remove them and make sure you are comfortable — you might want to take off your shoes for extra comfort.

After the physical relaxation, I will describe to you a beautiful tropical beach with palm trees. It is important that you imagine yourself on the beach that I describe rather than in a place that you have actually been; in other words, I would like you to *create* the beach scene as if it is a fantasy of a perfect beach *rather than having a memory* of a place you may have been to. While I'm describing this place in nature, it would be really helpful if you can imagine standing on the beach looking through your eyes at the scenery (i.e. what is referred to as "associated") as opposed to seeing yourself on the beach ("dissociated"). So please be in your body looking through your eyes each and every time you listen to this and any of the other sessions.

Once you are nicely relaxed on this gorgeous beach, I'm going to introduce some positive suggestions to you and your all-powerful subconscious mind. These suggestions address

19

the most common symptom of lacking confidence: getting nervous or anxious in situations where you are likely to be the focus of people's attention, or even feeling anxious just thinking about those situations (commonly referred to as "the fear of the fear"). These situations can range from formal presentations and big meetings to social events and even one-to-one encounters. The suggestions on the *Confidence Booster* session are about you remaining cool, calm and in complete control in any of those scenarios and expressing yourself confidently and positively at all times. My advice is to imagine (see and feel) that happening when you hear those suggestions, and perhaps imagine an actual upcoming "event" or "test" with you performing really well! Make those scenarios as "real" as possible. Then I will return you to the beach before the session ends in order to give you some positive affirmations before counting to ten and asking you to open your eyes. As hypnosis is a perfectly natural state, you will feel that you can open your eyes at any point during the session. This is normal and doesn't mean that you're not "hypnotized", it means that you are in complete control; hypnosis is, after all, a consent state — you allow yourself to relax because you want positive change. "All hypnosis is self-hypnosis" is a very common phrase in most teachings about hypnotherapy. In my experience, most clients feel so deeply relaxed that they don't want to break that state by opening their eyes. Imagine if you will that you are soaking in a luxuriously warm (and perhaps fragrant) bath at the end of a hard day's work. You're just getting relaxed and feeling good when after only a minute the telephone in the next room rings. Do you really want to get out of that bath to answer it? That's what it feels like if and when the thought to open your eyes enters your head when relaxing to the sessions.

To access this session you first need to register by going to www.humandoingandhumanbeing.com. Click on Reader Welcome and enter the following password: Love4Me Once you've completed registration, you will receive a confirmation email with instructions. If possible, please use headphones in order to optimize the effect.

## After listening for the first time

I hope you enjoyed that! I sincerely hope you relaxed well. If your body felt heavier or lighter, this is perfectly normal. I hope you found it easy for you to be "in your body" on the beach. With any luck you could imagine seeing the waves or the palm trees. Perhaps it felt like you could feel the sand beneath your feet or the warmth of the sun on your skin. It's rare, but some people report hearing the sound of seabirds when the only sound effect is the waves; or smelling or tasting the ocean air.

When I gave you suggestions about being able to do what you want to do, could you see that or sense that? Did you imagine yourself in scenarios where you were expressing yourself confidently? Some clients report having the sensation of tingling in their fingers but can't remember why! How long did that session seem to you compared to how long it actually was?

I would like you to play this session at least eight times before moving onto the next prescribed audio self-development session. You are advised to play this *Confidence Booster* session a minimum of once per day; twice a day is better, but leave at least four hours between plays — there is no benefit in playing any sessions too close together.

Very rarely, some clients report getting itches or wanting to scratch while listening to a session — please ignore these distractions because they soon pass!

I sincerely hope you have a similar experience to virtually all my clients who have experienced the *Confidence Booster* session. Most will report an immediate improvement in their confidence levels when faced with a "test" situation; others may give me third party references, such as *"I wasn't sure if anything had changed, but my partner commented on how relaxed and in control I was in handling a stressful situation with X."* Whether the improvements are experienced straightaway or not, you need to listen to the Confidence Booster session regularly for at least one week. Once you have played it eight times you can alternate between listening to it and the *Multi-Level De-Stressor* session, if that is your next session.

## CHAPTER FIVE
# *The Multi-Level De-Stressor*

Before listening to the *Multi-Level De-Stressor*, please read this chapter in order to prepare yourself for the positive changes that this powerful session can bring about for you emotionally, mentally, and even physically with health issues you may have.

There are so many circumstances in a person's life that this session can address, it is not just for the "stressed" individual. First of all, the *Multi-Level De-Stressor* enables you to process and deal with many years of accumulated layers of negative, harmful emotions lying beneath the level of your conscious awareness — this is why it can be said over time to have the power to deal with all your emotional baggage. It is widely acknowledged, even in the field of conventional medicine as well as increasingly by the general public, that there is a huge mind-body connection (psycho-soma), and that many "illnesses" have a psychological cause and thus have their roots in unresolved issues or "fixed" emotional states. Indeed, there is a whole industry dedicated to this field — check out the pioneering work since the 1980s of Louise L. Hay.

Therefore, as well as protecting you from the actual and potential effect of recent, current and future stressors, the *Multi-Level De-Stressor* allows you to get in touch with *and then consciously release* the emotional, and sometimes physiological (psychosomatic), effects of stressful incidents or traumatic events of the past. So many of my clients in recent years have chosen to avoid the chemical route offered by prescription medicines that is aimed only at the symptoms, in favour of holistic therapies that seek to resolve the cause of their ills or "dis-ease". That is why the *Multi-Level De-Stressor* is ideal for depressives and others who would benefit from releasing or processing more speedily longstanding and current negative emotional states (typically sadness, grief, anger, fear, guilt or frustration) that arise from bereavement, loss/separation, trauma, phobias, abuse, resentment, upsets, etc. Many of these may have manifested over time as so-called "stress-related", and other, conditions, e.g. IBS (irritable bowel syndrome — constipation, diarrhoea, spastic colon, etc.), skin disorders (eczema, psoriasis), ulcers, migraines, tumours, unexplained pain, panic attacks, anxiety, depression, weight gain; also, possibly sexual problems and eating disorders (bulimia, anorexia).

Secondly, the *Multi-Level De-Stressor* makes you more resilient and able to cope with any future stress by providing you with the means of empowering yourself to consciously move away from any negative emotional states that others may deliberately or unknowingly cause in you, so that you can within moments bounce back to a default positive state of being.

I cannot emphasize enough how self-empowering you can become by understanding the valuable pieces of information that follow and implementing them in your life.

*When emotions occur we automatically become a victim to them. Why is that? Because, up until now, no-one has taught us to react any differently!*

When someone says or does something to us that makes us feel sad, upset or angry, we may lash out, appropriately or inappropriately. More often than not though, we embrace the emotion and own it. We then suffer under the effect and affect of that emotion for as long as we keep thinking about what happened. What possible enjoyment or pleasure can most sane people gain from remaining in a negative state? Read further to discover in *How to Let Go* how you will now be able to control negative states and minimize their effect on you.

## Preparation

For this self-development session, I am going to utilize a more subtle method of relaxation that is designed to relax you deeper than the induction used in the *Confidence Booster*. This time I'm going to ask you to be aware of your muscles, and we'll be working from the top down starting with the face and the jaw. A lot of people experience tension and stress in the jaw, so you'll hear me asking you to part your teeth a little bit to relax your jaw. The relaxation will go into your temples, your forehead will smooth out, and your eyelids may feel heavy. We'll also relax your neck, back, chest, stomach and legs.

Then you'll imagine that you are walking down ten steps to the peaceful place in nature that I have prepared specifically for this session. Allow yourself to relax deeper as you walk down each step before you find yourself on a beach enjoying the changing colours of the sky as the sun sets. I need to remind you again to please be in your body on the beach looking out of it at the scene. Soon you will be lying on the beach looking at the full moon and the stars and listening to the waves — this scene in nature has been created especially and specifically to enable you to connect more easily with your emotions.

It's very important that when I ask you to allow and give permission for any underlying emotions to come up, that you don't force the process or try to make anything happen. This is very much a passive role! There will be a long gap of silence from me to give time for this process to happen — in that period of time you don't "do" anything! Just enjoy the comfort of your chair and imagine you are on this peaceful beach, while waiting to see what, if anything at all, comes up. If nothing surfaces the first time, that's perfectly fine, you can listen again the next day. Statistically, over 90% of my clients experience just one or two emotions coming up the first time; it's unlikely that your subconscious or higher self would bring to the surface more than a few emotions, it's usually the one or two that you can easily handle at any one time.

As to the type of emotions likely to come up, love, joy, peace, happiness, contentment and satisfaction are not likely to come up. That's not because you don't have any of them in your life, but since this is therapy it's much more beneficial that a "negative" emotion come up so that it can be released. Because of this, it's more likely that one or two of the following will surface: anger, bitterness, resentment, frustration, sadness, loneliness, guilt, grief, fear, jealousy, insecurity, rejection.

I'm going to give you some examples now of what to do and *How to Let Go*. Anger is one of the most common emotions to surface with this *Multi-Level De-Stressor* process, so I will use anger as an example. Let's assume that anger comes up for you when listening to the *Multi-Level De-Stressor* session. It could be anger from a situation that you're experiencing right now, or possibly anger from an incident that you'd almost forgotten about many years ago. Irrespective of where in time the anger originates, let's assume that you're still angry with that person about that situation and, if possible, you'd like to "have it out" with that person. Therefore, in order to do that, you have to keep the anger. So, the question arises, how do you keep the anger and/or any other emotion that comes up? The answer, very simply, is to *make a conscious decision to keep it.*

Continuing with this example, it's quite possible that when you listen to the *Multi-Level De-Stressor* session again a day or so later, that the same anger about the same person and the same situation comes up again, and whether you have "had it out" with that person or not, you may now be able to look at the whole situation with a different perspective — you may now be thinking *"Why am I keeping hold of this anger? It's not helping me at all, it's not serving any useful purpose."* So now you are ready to let go of it. So just how do you let it go? Some people think that because it is anger they have to fight it and do battle with it. No, you don't. *The key to letting*

29

*go is* **You wanting It to No Longer be there.** It's as simple as that. It may be difficult for many people to accept, especially when we are used to going into victim mode and wallowing in them whenever emotions occur, but *you control the emotions, not the other way round!* So please acknowledge it and decide *Don't need this anymore. Thanks, but no thanks!* You can tell it *Goodbye, Good riddance.* Or if you like, *You are the weakest link. You're fired, no longer required!* (or whatever other phrases work for you!)

Now let's say that anger does come up when you listen to the *Multi-Level De-Stressor* session today, and that you do decide to let it go by using the phrases above. Good job, but don't be too surprised if next time you listen to this session that it's back again. Why is that? Maybe that's because it's a "big" emotion, or one that you've been holding on to for a very long time, but usually if and when it does come back there's less of it — every time you let it go, you're getting rid of a big chunk at a time. That makes perfect sense, doesn't it?

It looks like I'm making out that anger is negative, and in a lot of cases it is, especially if it's an anger that has been suppressed or held onto over a long period of time — this, along with suppressed resentment and bitterness, will adversely affect your immune system and can lead to chronic conditions and the most serious life-threatening illnesses, including Cancer. (Toxicity is not solely environmental; negative thoughts, mindsets and attitudes are just as powerful in adversely affecting the health of our body.) However, some of my clients may happen to be in an abusive situation, possibly at home or at work. If their only defence against the abuse is the anger, then they would be fully justified in keeping hold of it — you don't want to take away their defences. Similarly, if a client has specifically come to see me in order to *get past* a previous relationship, usually an unhealthy one — it may be affecting all subsequent or potential relationships — then, as part of the *FOOL* (falling out of love) program, I would recommend to them that they let go of any love and keep hold of any anger that comes up for their ex-partner because, therapeutically, it's what is needed at the time to help them move on. If you don't fall into either of these two categories, then please take the opportunity to let go of anger and any other negative emotions that may surface for you whenever you play this session.

I can tell you that in 95% of cases when an emotion comes up, it will usually be experienced in the head because it is linked to a specific incident or a memory; but 5% of the time it can be experienced in the body, or in the head and the body. For example, the anger could be felt in your fists as if you want to punch somebody. Fear, as we all know, is usually felt in the stomach. Sadness, especially if the sadness is to do with grief, bereavement, loss or separation, tends to be felt around the heart chakra, an energy point in the centre of your chest. Now the thing about sadness is that some people believe that their only connection with, for example, the dead person is the sadness, and that if they decided to let the sadness go, they would be betraying that person. In my opinion, that is not so — if you let go of the sadness, it usually gets replaced with happier memories or happier feelings, which is what that person would want for you, yes? Now if you get a feeling of frustration and you experience it in the throat, then that's probably to do with *not having said something you really wanted to say* because the throat is all about communication.

This leads us nicely onto sensations. As well as or instead of emotions, some of you may experience physical sensations. So what should you do if you get a sensation — should you keep it or should you let it go? Once again, bearing in mind this session is a form of therapy, you are unlikely to experience many pleasant, agreeable sensations, apart from the obvious sensations of relaxation. On the other hand, if you experienced a stabbing pain, no matter how small, commonsense dictates you let it go, yes? However, if you get a sensation in between these two extremes of pleasant and unpleasant, or you're not sure, please please let it go! For example, you might experience what feels like a pressure on your chest, or your head, etc. that you might describe as *harmless, innocent, innocuous* or *neutral*. Even so, I strongly recommend you let it go. Why? Because I see many clients suffering from Irritable Bowel Syndrome who, when we do this session, experience sensations like that in the area of the stomach, and many of them make the decision to let them go. As a result, the vast majority of cases when they come back to see me report that their stomach and their digestion have improved dramatically! I also recall a particular client who suffered badly from severe migraines who in his session felt *"a tight band"* around his head which he decided to let go. Next time he came to see me, he said: *"I don't know what's happened but I haven't had a single headache!"* I looked at his notes and I said: *"Do you remember last time you were here, you got the sensation of a tight band around your head?"* *"Yes?"*

*"And you let it go?"* *"Yes?"* After a long pause he understood. I repeat, there is a huge mind-body connection, so if you are not sure, always let go. As far as I am concerned, you will never go wrong letting go of stuff, but you may not be doing the best for your health and well-being by keeping hold of stuff, so if in doubt, ALWAYS LET GO!

**N.B.** It may interest you to know that after listening to this *Multi-Level De-Stressor* session a few times, it should click with you that you can let go and process negative emotions *in real time*, i.e. at all other times, not just when listening to the session. For example, somebody in a work or social situation could say or do something to you that makes you feel upset, sad or angry; instead of thinking "I can't wait to get home and listen to the *Multi-Level De-Stressor* session, I'm sure I'll still be feeling like this in a few hours' time, then I can let it go", why not let it go there and then? Tell it *"Thanks but No thanks, etc, No Longer Required!"*

We have now covered the first part of the *Multi-Level De-Stressor* session, which is all about letting go of emotions and feelings that you may have been holding on to for a long, long time. The second part is the stress protector, and this is like having a shield, or force field, or protective bubble, all around you — inside the bubble / behind the shield, you're calm, you're relaxed, you feel safe, secure and in control. On the other side, people could be freaking out, they could be trying to throw their negative stuff at you, and it will just bounce off your protective device and away. I recommend you get a strong sense of that shield, energy field or bubble when I introduce it to you for the first time, and also every time you listen to the *Multi-Level De-Stressor* in order to reinforce it. We just don't know what life has in store for us. One day you could walk into a situation that you couldn't have foreseen would be that stressful, maybe even dangerous, and before you think "Oh my god, where's my protection?", instantly that shield or bubble will be there for you if you've practised it. So please make it real. I will then take you back to the beach for a sunrise before closing the session.

I strongly recommend you now read again all of this Preparation section before listening to the *Multi-Level De-Stressor* session for the first time as there is a lot of useful information to retain.

Go to www.humandoingandhumanbeing.com to access the session. If possible, please use headphones in order to maximize the effect.

## After listening for the first time

Most of my clients report relaxing more quickly and deeply when listening to this session than they did with the *Confidence Booster* session, so I hope you experienced that too. Did you visualize the full moon and the stars? Did it seem like you could you feel the warmth of the sand against your back? Did any emotions come up for you this first time? Did you feel them in any particular part of your body? Do you know what those emotions were about, or were they general rather than specific? Did you let them go?? Perhaps you experienced physical sensations that you didn't expect. You may be interested to know that when any of my anxiety/panic attack clients experience any of their nervous symptoms surfacing during this session, and they let them go, then those symptoms are 80% less likely to come up again in the future; and that's before doing the session that's designed to knock out all negative phobic reactions.

What did your shield or bubble look like? The most common feedback is that it looked like a perspex see-through bubble or egg-shape; that it felt *"good"* or *"safe"*; and that sometimes arrows or people or *"stuff"* couldn't get through or were bouncing off. Some clients report being protected by metal or Roman shields; others have energy fields *"like the force field in Star Trek"*.

I recommend to all my clients who listen to the *Multi-Level De-Stressor* session that they keep a Diary, and you might like to keep a record of your progress by doing the same. If so, here are the questions for your *Multi-Level De-Stressor* Diary:

## If Emotions came up

What emotion?

Who or what about?

Where, if anywhere, in the body?

Did you keep it or let it go?

If you let it go, did it go? (You may not know whether it has gone permanently, but did it go when you told it to or by the end of your session?)

## If Sensations came up

How would you describe the sensation?

Where in the body?

Is it familiar (one you've had before) or brand new (never experienced before)?

Did you keep it or let it go?

If you let it go, did it go? (You may not know whether it has gone permanently, but did it go when you told it to or by the end of your session?)

I recommend you listen to the *Multi-Level De-Stressor* session at least twelve times before moving on to the next audio self-development session recommended for you by the Self-Esteem Test. You should listen to this session once a day and certainly no more than twice in a day, with a minimum four-hour gap. If you are still enjoying listening to the *Confidence Booster* session, then you may want to alternate the two. If you do want to play both sessions in the same day, I would advise you to play the *Confidence Booster* session in the morning and the *Multi-Level De-Stressor* session in the evening when you are more likely to be in touch with your emotions. And don't forget that you can let go in real time and not have to remain in any negative emotional state for anywhere near as much time as you used to; and that you can consciously apply your shield/protective bubble before any intimidating interactions, whether face-to-face or over the phone.

## Postscripts on what can sometimes happen after listening to the *Multi-Level De-Stressor* session

Some listeners would appear to have a "delayed reaction" to this session, i.e. they may find an emotion like anger coming up for no reason that is relevant to the situation at the time, many hours after listening to the session. Be aware of this so that you can let go. Then note it in your Diary.

Other listeners are pleasantly surprised or amazed to experience relief and release from so-called chronic conditions. If you have good news then you are welcome to share it with me and other readers, via my website or Facebook.

In extremely rare cases, and probably because these clients are having inner child therapy with me, the subconscious feels the time is now appropriate to show flashbacks of incidents that the client does not consciously remember, painful episodes that have been locked safely away in the vaults of the subconscious. In the rare event that you start to experience flashbacks that you find puzzling, unexpected or distressing, then you really need the live one-to-one support of a professional therapist who can facilitate the therapy for which your subconscious is now priming you.

# CHAPTER SIX

# A Closer Look at Your Self-Esteem

## Self-Esteem Test #2

The guide time for completion is five to ten minutes.

This self-diagnostic tool looks at the conditioning we receive from our early days and how that programming from our main carers has made us who we are, with unwanted patterns of behaviour that we can only now begin to change. This self-analytical section, along with the one on Negative Self-Beliefs, allows you to bring that programming into conscious awareness so that you can choose to behave differently, in a similar way to how cognitive behavioural therapy (CBT) works. This would be very difficult to maintain and accomplish if not for the inclusion of the *Meet and Heal your Inner Child* self-development session which works on a very deep level to heal the past and raise your self-esteem.

*Your relationship with the world and yourself*

1.  Do you compare yourself unfavourably to others? Are other people "*better*" than you? Does that apply to co-workers, friends and even partners (past or present)?

2.  Do you hold back in letting new people get to know you? Is that because you think they would find you uninteresting or even boring? Or is it because you feel vulnerable — that they might take advantage of you, or even hurt you? And if you answered, as many of my clients have, that it was because "*They wouldn't like me*", then let me ask you "Why not? Why wouldn't they like you?" Most people cannot answer this question because the feeling of not being worthy of being liked is not a logical one; nevertheless, until this inner child is met and loved by you, it's a very powerful assumption, belief and conviction!

3.  Are you a people-pleaser? Do you find it difficult to say "no" to others? Consequently, do people at work, or even at home, "dump" on you? This fear of rejection (and, in some cases, abandonment, by partners or family) has its roots in your insecurities and not in reality! From this moment on, I would like for you, when somebody asks you to do something for them that you really do not want to do, to say "no" in the nicest possible way — in other words, to qualify it. For example: "I really would like to help you out Connie, but I'm so busy at the moment with _____. Can you ask somebody else please? In a couple of weeks I might

be available." Your fear is that the person who has been taking advantage of your kindness (low self-esteem?) for so long will reject you. Of course their initial reaction will be one of surprise because you have never said "no" before, but once you explain why you can't help them out this time, they will understand and accept your decision. Give it a go and see!

4. Do you hide your true feelings, especially when a person has said or done something to upset you or make you feel angry or sad? Do you say you're *"fine"* when you're not? Are you used to sub-serving your feelings, and perhaps even your needs, to those of others? In which case *"fine"* stands for "F***ing Incapable of Normal Expression"! Like a volcano, do you then "blow up" out of proportion to what's happening at the time because of the pressure of long held suppressed true feelings?

5. Do you attract needy, withdrawn or abusive partners? Is that a "safer" relationship, to feel needed, than a so-called "normal" relationship? Do you feel that you don't deserve a better relationship? If you have a history of partners who were abusive (usually mentally/emotionally, not just physically violent or sexually abusive) or alcoholic, did this in any way mirror your own parents' relationship?

6. Whenever a partner has told you that they loved you, have you been able to feel that love from them? Or do

you disbelieve them? Have you been able to feel love for them? If so, how easy has it been for you to tell them that you love them?

7. Do you feel that you disappoint others: your own family, your parents? Do you feel that you haven't met their expectations of you, or your own expectations of yourself? Have your parents actually told you, or made it clear to you, what their expectations of you were, or have you just assumed the burden of these *implied* expectations? What are these expectations that others have of you? What are yours, and what is the difference, if any, between the two? Whether those expectations are implied or explicit, are you ready now to let the burden, weight and pressure of them go?

All of the above are symptomatic of a childhood lacking security, approval or affection.

*How to Score Self-Esteem Test #2*

In each of the 7 categories, if you could identify with the first question and/or most of its content, award yourself points as follows:

1=2, 2=2, 3=3, 4=2, 5=3, 6=*2 points each* for the 3 categories of not being able to (a) feel love from, (b) and/or feel love for, or (c) express it; 7=2.

*Totals*

*0–3*   You require audio self-development sessions *1, 4 and 5*

*4–8*   Please listen to sessions *1, 2, 4 and 5*

*9–20*   Heal your childhood with sessions *1, 2, 3, 4 and 5* (N.B. For you, the following two chapters are essential reading!)

# CHAPTER SEVEN

# Sticks and Stones

*"Sticks and stones may break my bones,*
*But words will never hurt me."*
*(Oh really?)*

We are the accumulation of everything that has happened previously in our life: all the criticisms or negative comments, statements and experiences, especially those in our most formative years, our childhood. *We are a computer waiting to be programmed.* If a parent or primary carer tells us *"You're stupid," "Don't be an idiot,"* or *"You're useless,"* we believe it. Our parents are our Gods; if they say it, it must be true!

Of course abuse can be less or more subtle, as we shall explore later, but the effects are similar: a poor sense of self-worth that translates as insecurity in significant relationships despite compliments and regular reassurances, and a minimal level of expectations in life. This can manifest as low career aspirations and avoiding challenges, although interestingly

45

the opposite can also be true. Some people's deep unconscious drive to gain approval from their parents (usually from the father) means they will embrace any and every challenge, in search of the ever elusive, never attained "I'm proud of you."

What constitutes abuse? Prior to training as a hypnotherapist in 1990, I had always thought of "abuse" as referring mainly to sexual abuse. How wrong I was! Abuse ranges from the most obvious to the most subtle. Most of the time it is meted out unconsciously, having been learned and passed down from one generation to the next. In fact, there are times when a client will say to me, as if to defend the abuser: "It wasn't his fault. His father was a *strict disciplinarian / bit of a bastard / also an alcoholic / violent man / abuser, etc.*"

A classic example of Abuse comes from early in my career with one of my first inner child clients. John was a well-dressed, intelligent and very likeable young man presenting with self-esteem issues. He had ticked amongst other symptoms on his self-esteem check form *Feeling unworthy and avoiding challenges*. When I asked John for an example of this, he told me that as a team leader he would call a meeting of his team in order to discuss a new project he had devised. His co-workers would congratulate him on his ideas. At the end of the meeting he would then say "OK, who wants to take the lead on implementing it?" Their reaction would be one of disbelief, as if to say "But it's your baby, don't you want the credit?" He would say "No, that's alright, somebody else can do it." When he told me this, I found myself instinctively compelled to ask him for any particular memories from his childhood that stood out, and this is what he told me:

> *I remember coming home from school one day really happy. "Mum, Dad, guess what, I came top of the class!" Mum said: "Well done!" So, feeling good, I said: "Guess how many percent I got?" She said: "What percent did you get?" I said: "I got 97 percent!" and my Dad said: "What about the other 3 percent?"*

Talk about "pulling the rug from under his feet", or even "raining on his parade". For this child, his "script" was now going to include *"Whatever I do is never going to be good enough."* I am sure the father had never attained 97 percent in anything in his life, but even if he had, it made no difference, the damage was done. As Henry Wadsworth Longfellow (1807–1882), the American poet and educator, so accurately describes it: *"A torn jacket is soon mended; but hard words bruise the heart of a child."*

Let's now imagine another school child coming home that same day, feeling a little down… *"Mum, Dad, I came fifth, I got 76 percent."* Parents, picking up on his disappointment: *"That's OK son, what can we do to help you do better?"* This child is going to enjoy greater self-esteem and in all likelihood do better, and achieve more, in adult life! As the French philosopher Joseph Joubert (1754–1824) tells us with great clarity: *"Children need models rather than critics."*

To continue with the "coming home from school" theme, there may very well be a fortunate child who feels secure anyway and is less likely to feel that he or she has let anyone down, however well or comparatively badly he or she does at school. In my opinion, more damaging to a child's self-esteem than having huge expectations thrust on tiny shoulders, is when there are *no expectations* and *no interest* in the child's education or development. Neglect and disinterest by parents or main carers will foster major insecurity and huge self-doubt in the psyche of the child.

This leads us nicely onto the subject of what I call "passive abuse" — parents and carers please take note! Children need validation and approval all the time, even when you are busy. They need to know that their efforts are valued. So, for example, when my infant son or daughter presents me with the picture they have been drawing intensely for the last twenty or thirty minutes, I stop myself saying *"What is it?"*, or at least preface it with *"Wow, darling / gorgeous / sweetheart, that's brilliant / wonderful! I love the colours. And is that a butterfly / dog / firework I can see there?"* (This is pure guesswork from me, hoping I've got it right.) The response will usually be: *"Daddy, you're funny. Can't you see it's Mommy / a giraffe / an elephant?"*

Hugs, kisses and cuddles are tangible evidence to us as children that we are loved. And so is interest by parents in our activities and accomplishments. All this contributes to a greater sense of security in us as to our place in the family and in the world. Enjoying such good self-esteem, we are more likely to flourish socially and in the challenging environments of school and the world. On the other hand, lack of affection or interest, and even critical comments or unfavourable comparisons, even if unintended, will undermine any confidence we may have had. These can be as unsubtle as *"Why can't you be more like your brother?"* (or *"I wish you'd never been born!"*, or even *"You were a mistake."*) to the almost complimentary *"Well done on getting an 'A' and 2 'B's... Did you know your brother / sister / cousin / neighbour's children got 3 'A's?"*

Many of us become "stereotyped" by our parents, and thus forever restricted in our potential to achieve or enjoy genuinely earned success. Many is the time I have heard clients tell that a sibling is their mother or father's favourite, e.g. "the blue-eyed boy". In one client's family, her brother was "the clever and intelligent one". The parents had few expectations of her, especially academically. The brother was, to quote the proud mother, "the one who went to university". His younger sister, my client, also did well academically and actually studied at Cambridge University, one of the top two British universities, but this was never mentioned. Even though she achieved a top-class honours degree, the damage had already been done, thanks to the negative conditioning and programming throughout her childhood. Whenever she had sat any entrance exams and tests, or handed in course work, and in most cases received top marks, she always thought there had been a mistake in the marking or that she had fluked it. (How could they be her results? It was her brother who was the intelligent one!)

Abuse is more insidious than you would think, and I purposely include more real-life examples in the following chapter in order to make you wonder about your own upbringing, and thereby stimulate and prepare your inner child for your eventual meeting and healing. In the meantime, ponder the musings in his wry observation on Family of twentieth century English poet Philip Larkin (1922–1985) in this famous verse.

## This Be The Verse

*They fuck you up, your mum and dad.*
*They may not mean to, but they do.*
*They fill you with the faults they had*
*And add some extra, just for you.*

*But they were fucked up in their turn*
*By fools in old-style hats and coats,*
*Who half the time were soppy-stern*
*And half at one another's throats.*

*Man hands on misery to man.*
*It deepens like a coastal shelf.*
*Get out as early as you can,*
*And don't have any kids yourself.*
(Philip Larkin)

To further empower you, by making you consciously aware of your programming, we are now going to look at *negative self-beliefs* (Negs). These are conscious and unconscious beliefs you have about yourself that automatically come into play in certain scenarios or situations. Up until now, you have probably had no control over them, so they have robbed you of your power and prevented you from enjoying your life to its full potential. Identifying your own negs, and recognizing when they come up, is the first step to empowering yourself to consciously override your programming and conditioning, and to then react in more positive, healthy and fulfilling ways.

Below is a list of some negative self-beliefs. First of all, I'd like you to consider each one carefully and write down on a blank sheet of paper the ones that are really familiar to you, ones with which you can identify very strongly. Don't worry if you find yourself writing down many — there will be "crossovers". For example, there is one situation which for many of my clients will result in many negs; some of them even contradict each other. I will reveal what that common situation is once you have taken your time and carefully thought about each one.

The guide time for completing your list of negs is five to ten minutes, but please take more time if you need it.

## *Negative Self-Beliefs*
(→ conscious awareness → positive options )

People hurt me

I can't trust men

I can't trust women

I don't belong

Nobody wants me

I'm unlovable

I'm bad

I'm useless

I'm unworthy

I'm dirty

I'm not right

I'm a disappointment

I can't

I can't do it

I can't get enough

I can't get started

I can't finish anything by myself

I'm not here

Nobody notices me

My love hurts others

I'm a nuisance

I'm misunderstood

I'm different

I'm overlooked

I don't exist

It's not worth it

It's not my fault

I can't get out

I have to get out of here

I have to be angry to survive

I need pain to survive

I need illness to survive

I'm not good enough

I'm worthless

I'm stupid

I'm not worth it

I'm the wrong one

I'm weak, I'm helpless

I have to do everything alone

I don't want to be here

I can't get through

Nothing works for me

I don't know

Nobody listens to me

I'm in the way

I'm cut off, I'm separate

I'm second best, a substitute

I'm less important

They are wrong

It's not fair

I'm powerless

Do you now have a complete list of the negs that apply to you? If you do, I want you to now go through your list, taking one neg at a time, and ask yourself: *"When do I get this?"* Answering this should take you at least twice as long as it took you to select your negs.

Write down next to each one the situations that bring up that neg. Additional questions that you could ask before *When do I get this?* for specific negs could be:

I'm not right
Q: Does "I'm not right" mean you are not well, or that you are wrong?

I can't finish anything by myself
Q: Does this mean that you don't finish it, or that other people have to help you finish it?

I'm different
Q: Is that good that you are different? Or bad? Or both (i.e. that you would like to be more acceptable to people)?

It's not worth it
Q: What's not worth it?

I have to be angry to survive
I need pain to survive
I need illness to survive
Q: Is this a "script" that has been learnt from childhood, one that was taught you by a parent or main carer?

I have to do everything alone
Q: Is that good or bad? (Usually "bad" because most people want a special someone with whom to share their life.)

They are wrong
Q: Who are they?

The one specific situation that I was referring to when I mentioned multiple negs is that of being with people, e.g. in groups, and it can bring up negs that would appear to be contradictory such as *Nobody notices me* and *I'm a nuisance.*

Now that you have listed the scenarios which cause you to give away your power by repeating, and thereby confirming and reinforcing, your negative self-beliefs, it's time for you to break the program! Do you not realize that you go into some of those situations, especially the group scenario, *projecting* your negs so that others respond accordingly! Just like self-fulfilling prophesies, your negative views of yourself and of the relationships others have with you, get reinforced again and again. To break that unconscious habit, all it takes is for you to *now be conscious and aware that you are about to do it!*

Your conscious awareness in those situations offers you the opportunity to react more positively. You need to "catch on" to stop yourself from automatically entering negative mode — remember, even if some of these negative self-beliefs you have are based on actual events in the past, it does not mean that you shouldn't hope for better outcomes from similar situations in the future.

Of course, this is only the first step, and at best only a temporary measure, if you are looking for positive changes that are deep and lasting. For you to achieve a huge shift from negative to positive in how you think and react, and a welcome divorce from victim mentality, will require the fulfilment, love and healing that arise naturally and easily from meeting your inner child at different times of need in his or her life. The aim of the next section is to prepare you for the *Meet and Heal your Inner Child* session.

# CHAPTER EIGHT
## *Your Story*

This chapter continues the process of self-reflection and self-analysis, and is an essential prerequisite for the next self-development session. The questions I ask you here are designed to stimulate the inner child inside of you in preparation for your meeting. In other words, she or he will be emotionally *raw* (**r**eady **a**nd **w**aiting for you) if you have taken the time to answer my questions.

To help you with your answers, and also to jog your memory, I have supplied sample answers from some of my clients. Their story may be different to yours, but the symptoms of a childhood lacking in love, affection or approval are easily recognizable.

## Part One

What are the memories that stand out for you in your childhood, good and bad? It will benefit you to just write down these memories as titles or headings, with perhaps sub-headings of how that made you feel, e.g.

*My Grandma who loved me died and I wasn't told for months*
 – *I resented their not letting me go to the funeral*
 – *I wanted to say Goodbye!*

*The sound of my father and mother arguing / fighting*
 – *Always made me feel afraid*
 – *Hated my father's drinking*
 – *I used to cry into my pillow*

Then provide an insight into the family dynamic, and please write these down too; doing so will ensure a more powerful and healing encounter with your inner child the first time you meet. For example, how would you describe the relationship between Mom and Dad? Were they ever affectionate towards each other? Which of the two was the major disciplinarian, and how would you be disciplined, and for what exactly? What, if any, were their most used negative comments, criticisms or put-downs? Did either parent treat any of your siblings any differently to you? Did you feel wanted? How did you get on with siblings? What was the atmosphere like in the home? If physical demonstrations of love and affection towards you were rare from parents/ main carers, did you receive it from any other relatives, e.g. grandparent, uncle or aunt?

Were you and/or your siblings allowed to have friends round to play, or were you too embarrassed about your parents or the state of the house to invite them over? Were there any potential friends you were discouraged from having by either of your parents, and why? If you were allowed to have friends round, did your parents behave differently in company? More importantly, did you ever go round to friends' houses? How was it there compared to your home? How different were their parents to yours and especially in the way they interacted with each other, with their kids, and with you? Is that the first time you realized that not all families were the same, and that maybe something was lacking at your home?

School/education. How did you get on at your different schools, with the teachers and with the other student? How did you perform academically? Were you ever called names or bullied at school? How interested in your education were your parents/main carers? Did they attend PTA meetings? Did they check you were doing your homework, or were you left to yourself? Was there much expectation of how well you should do, or none at all? Were there any classes or out-of-school activities you really wanted to do but were denied? If so, what reasons were given, and did those reasons also apply to any other siblings?

Were birthdays / Christmas / achievements celebrated? Were you ever left disappointed by what you were given or not given? Did a parent ever fail to keep a promise? Was praise easy to come by or in short supply? Were family holidays enjoyable or did something usually happen to spoil them?

## Part Two

This next exercise is ideally taken just before you play the *Meet and Heal your Inner Child* session, therefore about one hour should be set aside to cover both. If for any reason you cannot do both together, then all you need to do before you play the *Meet and Heal your Inner Child* session is to spend a few minutes reviewing your answers to this exercise.

I am going to be asking you direct questions about your childhood. All the questions start with "In your life, especially as a child, has anything been ……?" Please write down your answer to each question, and after each answer ask yourself the next appropriate question, typically "What?" and/or "By whom?" For example, for HOPED ("In your life, especially as a child, has anything been HOPED?"), it could be you that was doing the hoping, or someone else — usually when "it" was being done to you, it was usually by a Mother or Father, or both.

MADE WRONG is a more popular way of saying "invalidated". To use a real life example from one of my clients, Mike's father never attended any PTA meetings or met with any of Mike's teachers. Dad did however accompany Mike to school for the prize-giving evening. After a while, Mike's name was called out and he went up on stage to receive his award. The applause was just tailing off as he sat back in his seat. Mike recalls his father turning to him to speak. Mike is expecting him to say how proud he is of him; instead Dad says: "I am so embarrassed, I wish you'd got your hair cut." For Mike, this whole celebration of his achievements was *made wrong* by his father.

When you go through this exercise, one or more answers may come up for a particular question. If this is the case, please give me the earliest example. It is perfectly OK to give me more than one answer at a time, if you prefer, however I will be wanting you to go through this process two times anyway. You may need one or two sheets of blank paper for your answers.

First Round

In your life, *especially as a child,* has

anything been SUPPRESSED

WITHHELD

MADE WRONG

ASSERTED

HOPED

HATED

DENIED

BORING

LOST

REGRETTED

SAID

IMAGINED

QUESTIONED

DISAGREED

AROUSED

SPOILT

FEARED

In your life, *especially as a child,* has

there been   NO COMMUNICATION

anyone been   LOVED

anything been   LOVED

For the second round, I am hoping you will come up with different answers — sometimes the second time reveals another layer deeper than the first, but don't worry if it's only the same answers that come up. In order to help you out, I will be revealing some of the answers I have received over the years. Like the host of *Family Fortunes* (or would *Family Misfortunes* be more accurate?), I will be giving you some of the top answers given to me over the years by inner child therapy clients.

## Second Round

In your life, *especially as a child,* has anything been SUPPRESSED?

The most popular answer here is "Emotions."
Whose emotions? "Mine."
By whom? "Me."
In truth, for the majority who answered this way, it wasn't you who was suppressing their emotions, it was your parents, and because there was a culture of non-expression of emotions and feelings in the family, you had no choice but to suppress yours too.

Other answers include "Me." "My personality / spontaneity / creativity… by my parents."

In your life, *especially as a child*, has anything been WITHHELD?

Top answer here is "Love and affection."
By whom? Usually "Mom and Dad."
"That I was adopted."

In your life, *especially as a child*, has anything been MADE WRONG?

Top answers include "Everything I said.", "Everything I did was made wrong by him / her." and "Me — I was always made wrong by him / her / them."

In your life, *especially as a child*, has anything been ASSERTED?

"My father's authority."

In your life, *especially as a child*, has anything been HOPED?

"No, nothing was ever hoped for me by my parents."
"That my father / mother would stop the drinking / fighting / arguments."
"That we could be a normal family."

In your life, *especially as a child*, has anything been HATED?

"My father." "School." "The bullies." "I hated myself, because I was told I should never have been born."

In your life, *especially as a child,* has anything been DENIED?

"Music / dancing lessons." "Toys." "Going to Grandma's funeral." "Approval." "Praise." "The abuse."

In your life, *especially as a child,* has anything been BORING?

"School." "Sundays." "Sunday school." "The holidays." "No, because I was always worried about what would happen next." (e.g. violence by father.)

In your life, *especially as a child,* has anything been LOST?

"My childhood." "My innocence." "My Grandpa." "My dog."

In your life, *especially as a child,* has anything been REGRETTED?

"My being born — by my mother / by me." "Not being born to a different family."
One client regretted that his cruel father hadn't died when my client as a teenager had made him a drink of tea with lots of belladonna in it — he was still upset about this failure many years later as he was telling me about it!

In your life, *especially as a child,* has anything been SAID?

"That I was a mistake — by my Aunt / mother / father."
"That I will never amount to anything — by a teacher."

In your life, *especially as a child,* has anything been IMAGINED?

"Peace, tranquility — that one day I wouldn't live in fear all the time." "What it would be like to have a happy childhood." "Friends." "That my father would come back and that we would be a happy family."

In your life, *especially as a child*, has anything been QUESTIONED?

"Everything I said / everything I did — by my mother / father." "No, I didn't dare to question anything because I would be hit."

In your life, *especially as a child*, has anything been DISAGREED?

See 'QUESTIONED' above.

In your life, *especially as a child*, has anything been AROUSED?

"Fear, of father." "Anger about my situation."

In your life, *especially as a child*, has anything been SPOILT?

"My whole childhood was spoilt." "Christmases. He always came home drunk from the pub and threw the meal against the wall." "My friendships. Every time I'd made a friend / got settled into a new school, we had to move house again."

In your life, *especially as a child*, has anything been FEARED?

"My father / brother." "Speaking out." "Waking up not knowing if my mother was alive or dead (from father's drunken brutal attacks)."

In your life, *especially as a child*, has there been NO COMMUNICATION?

"No, none whatsoever." "None after I told them I was pregnant." "Not between father and mother." "No love, affection or tenderness was ever communicated, only violence, anger and desperation."

In your life, *especially as a child*, has anyone been LOVED?

"My brother / sister — by my parents."

In your life, *especially as a child*, has anything been LOVED?

"My dog / doll." "Sport / music." "Our first house — I was happy there."

Coming back to the present time now, WHO DO YOU LOVE?

As well as "my partner, close friends", I hope that there are children on your list — hopefully your own children or your grandchildren, if you have any; if not, then perhaps young nieces or nephews, godchildren, or friends' children. This will be helpful for the next session. If, despite your childhood, you have put your parents on this list, then please remove them as it would not be appropriate to use them in the session.

Now that you have completed Round Two of this exercise, you are almost ready to meet your inner child and begin the process of deep healing that will transform your self-esteem, how you relate to others, and what you deserve to receive into your life.

# CHAPTER NINE

# Heal Your Childhood, Transform Your Life!

Please take a few moments to review your answers to the last exercise before preparing to meet your inner child.

For this *Meet and Heal your Inner Child* session, I will be using a similar relaxation induction to the one you enjoyed in the *Multi-Level De-Stressor* session. Then there will be ten golden steps taking you into a special garden which I call "the Beautiful Secret Garden". Inside the garden will be thousands of flowers, some butterflies, and birds singing.

I will take you through the garden until you are sat in a very comfortable chair where you can imagine relaxing more. Soon after, I will ask you to invite your inner child to be there with you. It's quite possible that she or he might already be there. Once the child is there, I'm going to ask you questions about the child that you won't need to answer until after the session, questions like *What's s/he wearing? What expression's on her/his face — is s/he happy, is s/he sad?* I'll ask you to check her/his body language: *Is s/he open? Is s/he closed?* At that time, make a mental note so that you can include that information in the inner child diary that I will be recommending you keep in order to monitor your progress. Do not be at all surprised when you meet your inner child for the very first time that she or he is very young, sad, withdrawn or closed off. This is very common! You can be comforted by the knowledge that, as you continue to listen to this session over the next few weeks, your inner child will become older and happier, which is the opposite of what most people remember about their childhood — most people would say that they were happier at the age of 5 than at 15. It's because of all the loving and healing that takes place in this session that your inner child becomes older and happier. Sometimes she or he may come through and give you advice or guidance about a situation that you are going through in your life at the time; in this respect this experience can be said to be similar to connecting with your higher self.

I will be asking you to make friends with your inner child. "Making friends" means physical contact, so depending on your inner child's size or age, that may mean picking her or him up to put on your lap or to sit next to you on your chair, or coming down to the child's level to give her or him a hug. I want you now to promise that you will do this! And if your inner child happens to be moody or sulking, please don't fall into the ego trap of *Well if you don't want to know me I don't want to know you!* That's not going to be helpful to anyone. If she or he is sulking, then that means that your inner child is probably hurting, and more than anything will want some attention, or somebody (you!) to make things right.

Then there are three basic questions I'm going to suggest that you ask your inner child, and these are: *What can I do to help you feel better? What are your needs?* and *What information do you need to give me?* And if there is an obvious question, please go ahead and ask it. So if for example your inner child is tearful, a good question would be *Why are you crying?* or *What are those tears for then?* So don't be afraid to ask any obvious questions, but the three recommended questions will usually bring up in your inner child an issue that you can address and help to resolve for her or him.

If your inner child doesn't want to talk to you, by the way, that's OK. If that's the case, you may be able to look at or into the child and know exactly what's going on for that child. It's not that you've had to go back in time in your head and access a memory, it's just that you can often tell simply by looking at the child *S/he's sad, S/he's lonely,* or *S/he's scared.* Hopefully the questions you ask will bring about a conversation and your inner child will give you her/his story. When I get you to ask those questions, there will be a long gap (just as in the *Multi-Level De-Stressor* session) and it's your role to give your inner child answers to those questions that will comfort and satisfy. So if your inner child asks *Why doesn't my mommy spend any time with me?*, you wouldn't say *Well she's really busy you know, looking after the house and you and your brother.* You would say *I've got all the time in the world, what do you want to do?* So it's very important that you answer your inner child's questions EMOTIONALLY, not intellectually. If she or he asks *Why doesn't my Dad love me?*, you wouldn't say *Well he's got real problems, he just doesn't know how to love,* you would say **I** *love you.* If your inner child says *I* *want a mommy or a daddy that loves me.* — *I'll be the mommy, I'll be the daddy that loves you.* If your inner child says *I haven't got any friends.* — *I'll be the bestest friend you ever had.* Your inner child might just want somebody to spend time with her or him, which I would encourage you to do. Whatever needs your inner child has, your role really is to ***fulfil those needs on an emotional level***. In this way, as you continue listening to this session daily and meeting and healing your inner child, it will be as if you are taking a time machine back to a moment of need in your childhood and plugging that gap, fulfilling that need, again and again and again…

You might like to prepare yourself to meet and heal your inner child by reading this chapter again. Then go to www.human doingandhumanbeing.com to access your gender-specific session. I have had clients who were post-op and pre-op transsexuals who were more comfortable with their inner child being addressed as the opposite gender to that which society would expect. If you are in a similar situation, you decide whether it is authentic and more comfortable for you to listen to the Male or Female session. Once again, I strongly recommend you use headphones. Also, I normally place a pillow or cushion on the chest of my clients so that they can give their inner child or themselves a hug if needed during their time together, so please use one for your session.

## After listening to the *Meet and Heal your Inner Child* session: *The Inner Child Diary*

I strongly recommend you keep an Inner Child Diary to chart your progress with the *Meet and Heal your Inner Child* session. From time to time you may want to review this Diary to check that you are giving the best response you can to meet your inner child's needs. The most important thing to bear in mind whenever you listen to this session is to answer your inner child's questions and needs *emotionally*, not intellectually!

Before moving on to the *Supreme Performance and Self-Esteem Booster* session, you need to have played your *Meet and Heal your Inner Child* session **at least twenty-four times**. You need only play this session once a day, and if you experience a particularly emotional time with your inner child, then it would be advisable to play the *Multi-Level De-Stressor* session next before you resume listening to the *Meet and Heal your Inner Child* session. Whenever you play two sessions in the same day, always leave a gap of at least four hours. Each time you play this inner child session, please take the time to write in your Diary everything that happened in your meeting. My advice is to do this immediately, and to allow that information to flow freely. Only after you have finished your account should you then check to see if you have included the following information; in other words, do not look at these questions as your starting point — if you do, then your inner child diary accounts will be short and dry rather than meaningful and memorable, and they won't be as pleasurable to read weeks, months or years later.

*HOW OLD* was your inner child?

Was s/he *HAPPY or SAD? OPEN or CLOSED?*

*EVERYTHING COMMUNICATED* between the Child and you, *whether spoken or not*.

Do you hold the Child, and *what effect* does this have?

Any *last message*?

*How does the Child feel* at the end? (i.e. *what change*, if any, e.g. "less sad" or even "happy"?)

*How do you feel* at the end? (Was it emotional for you?)

*Anything else* about your time together? (Did you and your inner child play together / pick flowers / look at the fish / ride on a swing, etc?) For one of my clients, the garden developed a boating lake so that she could take her inner child for a punt on the lake. Another businessman client who was very analytical, left-brained and sceptical about having this therapy, encountered a unicorn in the garden in his first inner child session!

Sometimes, despite your reassurances that you will be returning, your inner child will not want you to leave. There is a solution to this which I will share with you later rather than right now, in case it jeopardizes the effectiveness of most of your early experiences with your inner child. The best advice I can give you for now is to reassure your inner child that you will be coming back and that she or he is perfectly safe in the beautiful secret garden until then.

The importance of the inner child diary is enormous. It shows you the progress you are making. As mentioned in the Preparation for the *Meet and Heal your Inner Child* session, it is usual for the inner child to become older and happier, *contrary to what most people remember* about their childhood. This is as a result of all the loving and healing that occurs as you resolve the inner child's concerns. I have always dedicated a session especially to the Inner Child Diary before the *Supreme Performance and Self-Esteem Booster* session at which the client and I go through their Diary — to check that they are "doing it right"; but it's usually also a wonderful session for me to witness the power of the inner child therapy, and the positive and heart-warming changes the client is reporting. As an holistic therapist who is passionate about improving the self-esteem and quality of life for others, I am fortunate to be rewarded with many joyful accounts of the positive changes and transformations that are taking place in the lives of clients once they have embarked on their journey of self-healing. Some of mine and my trainees' best and most satisfying times are when a client returns after four weeks of playing their inner child CD with their inner child diary. The changes reported by the client in his or her outlook and expectations of life are the inspiration and fuel I need to continue as a therapist and trainer!

I have the permission of two of my thousands of clients to share their inner child diaries. They start after their first Inner Child live session with me which I recorded onto audio tape for George and onto a CD for Rita so that they could continue their inner child therapy at home. I am grateful to these clients for allowing me to reproduce their diaries within the pages of this book. Their names have been changed for reasons of confidentiality. I use my clients' and the UK's system of dating. This means, for example, that 1/3/98 is the 1st of March 1998 and not the 3rd of January 1998.

## George's Story

George was born and raised in Cyprus. His mother had married in her teens a man who turned out to be violent and alcoholic. When she finally separated from this monster she replaced him with another violent alcoholic. Life for the young George was far from good. I still remember to this day George telling me how as a young boy he sat down in the middle of a busy road praying for a truck to kill him and release him from his misery.

The initial reason George gave for coming to see me was that he was still suffering from the emotional fall-out of the unexpected break-up of a relationship in which he had invested his heart and soul, and he found it very difficult to move on. I can tell you that after therapy (including a Soul Retrieval session during which he and his ex-partner amicably returned each other's heart), George discovered his true soul mate within six months (see diary entries 1/3/98 and 16/3/98). They married within the year and enjoy a happy life together in the USA.

## George's Inner Child Diary

### Sunday 15/2/98

I saw the fountain, in the middle of the garden, this time it was grey and not white as I had first seen it.

My inner child appeared, he was about two to three years old, wearing a white dress. Then he changed to be about four to five wearing a cream jacket and trousers, with very curly hair like my mother always had mine when I was a child. He seemed lost, just standing there with a blank expression on his face, not open, just sad.

I picked my inner child up and put him on my lap. He said he was scared and lonely. I told him I was there to help him, he was safe with me, and that I would give him all the love he needs and that he need not be scared. I remember feeling so much for him, I knew how he was feeling, and I knew his every need. I told him he was very special and strong, and he will grow up to be positive and be happy. He said that couldn't be him, and I said it was him, he had all that and more.

I felt so much, I could relate to him so much, to this child. All I want to do is give him love and be there for him. I told him he could always come to this special place, and that I'll always be there for him.

I hugged him and it felt so good, I knew he would grow up to be someone and be happy.

## Tuesday 17/2/98

The fountain was white this time as I had seen it the very first time. There were streams of white lace flowing around it like it was a dream. I looked into the fountain and saw all the fish and all the colours criss-crossing through the water.

My inner child appeared as before, first as a happy child of three to four dressed in white, dancing and playing around the grass. He then changed to be about five to six, with curly hair wearing a cream jacket and trousers. Again he looked very sad and this time he had dirt on his face. I called him over to me and I picked him up, put him on my lap. I told him he was very special and that I was here to give him all the love he needed, and that he was safe.

I told him not to be sad anymore, that he was very special, and that everyone loved him and cherished him.

I took his hand and went for a walk in the garden. I told him to look at the beautiful flowers in the magic garden, how wonderful they were, just like him.

He said "Mum doesn't love me." I said "She does, very, very much." Then he said "Dad doesn't love me." I said "No, but I love you, I'm there for you."

I picked him up and hugged him, I told him that he was so very special, and never to forget that. I told him that people will always say "How special you are," and "You will be strong and happy, even when things go wrong you will always be strong." He said that I should be strong too, and I told him I was.

I cried and hugged him and felt all the love pass between us, tears trickled down my face there and for real.

I told him I will always be there for him, he could always come to the garden, and it was our magic garden.

I let him go, and told him to be strong.

I awoke with tears streaming down my cheeks. I felt that we had bonded, that healing had taken place. After all these years I was beginning to heal myself.

## Thursday 19/2/98

I felt warmth in the palms of my hands. My inner child appeared this time five to six looking happier, with a smile and more relaxed.

I told him he looked happier, and I was there to look after him, and be there for him.

I picked him up and put him on my lap, he smiled. I told him he was very special, and asked what could I do for him, how could I help him? He told me he wanted to play, I said "OK" and then he looked at me and said "Please don't be sad." I said "I'm not sad, I wish we had become friends a long time ago."

We played on the grass, hopscotch, football, rolling around. I told him that he will be good at anything he does, any sport, any hobby, anything; that he will have confidence and be positive, he can do anything he wants to do. I picked him up and hugged him, I felt all the love in the world, we were one, I was him and he was me, I was healing myself, I was loving myself. I told him I'd always be there for him.

When it was time to leave he looked at me and said "Remember to always be strong." I said I was and he went.

It seems as if I'm trying to heal my inner child and he's trying to heal me. He knows my feelings, my hurt, and me as much as I do his.

## Saturday 22/2/98

A child appeared dressed in a white tee shirt with multi-coloured dungarees on, he was about three to four. Then my inner child appeared, eleven to fifteen, dressed in a brown suit.

He looked sad; I told him he was safe, that I was there to look after him. What could I do for him, was there anything I could help him with? He said he couldn't go on with all the trouble at home, all the fighting, and the arguing. He said he was scared, and asked why him? Why does he have to be him? Why does he have to go through it all?

I reached out for him, I told him I knew exactly how he felt, but it was going to be alright. What was happening to him wasn't his fault; he was strong and will get over anything. That one day it will be all over, that he was normal, he doesn't have to be anyone else, because people will love him, and get on with him. He was special and is loved very much.

He looked on and I hugged him. I told him that this secret garden was there for him and me. That this is where he could always come to feel safe, happy and find me, I'll always be there for him. That we were one, we can face anything in life.

I knew exactly how he felt, every feeling, every fear, and every moment of every day. I've been there but I didn't want it to destroy him like it did me. I wouldn't let that happen to him. My feelings started to come back to me, the fear etc., but I fought them off, they can no longer hurt me.

My inner child said to me "Don't let me be alone", I said "Never because we are one."

At times I used to think I was going mad. I used to hide in my daydreams, hide away from reality, and I didn't want to have to face any problems ever again. I know that I have kept doing this in my adult years too. Now I am dealing with them, I will be stronger and better for doing this.

## Thursday 26/2/98

My inner child appeared to me smiling and happy. He was about eleven to twelve wearing his black school blazer with the yellow emblem of my old school *A... B... (in England)*. I told him he was safe, and that I was there to help him, give him love and attention.

He said he wished he could grow up, be like all the other grownups, he didn't want to be a child. He wanted to be able to do what he wanted. I told him that he would have plenty of time to do that, and that now he should play and enjoy his childhood. He was now in secondary school and that was scary for him. He felt alone but had made friends.

He said that deep inside he was scared of everything. Who was going to look after him? I said I would, and that being scared wasn't a bad thing. He told me he wanted to grow up to be like me, and I said that he would and he'll be happy. He will have everything that he wants, that life wouldn't always be easy, but that made it all the more worthwhile.

I told him that everyone loves him. Look how all the teachers look after him, he was special and would always be.

I gave him a hug and told him I would always be there for him. I knew how he felt, that we were one, and that we were both happy.

For most of my life that inner part of me, that child, has longed to be loved. Longing not to be alone, longing to be someone. He has always been locked away inside me. The feelings have always been with me, the feelings have always been with me through my adult years. I feel that my feelings were mine and I couldn't express them, that no-one would ever know how I felt or what I've been through or still am. My inner child has always wanted to let his feelings out, to cry out, and to scream out: his and my feelings, the anger, the hate, the loneliness, the sorrow, the self-pity and more.

Why can't I be strong, positive and have more confidence in myself? I want so much out of life, part of me wants it all, but part of me puts me down, part of me thinks I'm not good enough.

I have always felt intimidated by others. Always felt second best and I know that's wrong. But one day soon I'm going to be someone, I'm going to enjoy life. I'm fed up of being lonely, unhappy, I want to smile again.

### Saturday 28/2/98

My inner child appeared smiling, looking happy, eleven to twelve. He had his school blazer on and was very open.

He said he was happy to be back. I told him he was always welcome here, this is where he could always come to be loved and wanted. I told him I was glad to see him.

I asked him what I could do for him, he said he was lonely, no one understood him. He asked why he couldn't be like grownups, he wants to be like them. I said why and he said because they can do what they like, they're not told what to do, they're not scared. I told him that even grownups have problems too. He said why he can't be someone else, he didn't want to be George. Why couldn't he be different? I said because he was special that's why, that one day he would understand that being someone else doesn't make all the problems go away. That he should be happy to be who he is, strong, happy, loved.

We walked on the grass; I told him that life was about learning, about facing problems, facing life. That I was always there for him, we were one, that I knew him so well. He smiled, feeling better.

Before he left I asked if he had a message for me. He said yes. "You're special too" he said and I felt a tear run down my cheek.

I'm finally able to face my self, my inner child, it's so wonderful. The love I feel towards him is so strong. I know his every want, his every need, his every thought. Seeing him smile and leave happy makes me feel strong, makes me feel good about myself, I'm healing myself. I told him I'll always be there for him, and that I'll see him soon.

Someone does love George, someone does need George and that is me. To finally begin to love myself is a wonderful feeling. Love, compassion, hope, understanding and strength are all within me. I am beginning a new discovery, I'm finding me.

## Sunday 1/3/98

My inner child appeared, he was about fourteen to fifteen, wearing his black school blazer, but not as open as the last time.

I told him it was good to see him again, that he was welcome and safe, this is where he will always find love and someone who will look after him. I told him to come over and sit by me which he did. I said "You look happy." He said he was, he was doing better at school and getting on better. I told him that was good, because he could do anything he wanted to do, he was very special and never to forget that.

I asked him if he had any message for me, he said that Yaya (my Nan) was looking after me. I said she's looking after you too and we smiled.

We went for a walk on the grass, and I told him that this garden was so very special. He said "Yes" just like when he daydreams. He asked me if I daydream and I said "Yes I still do", and that it was OK. But to remember that he was strong, positive and enjoyed life, that was important.

When leaving I asked if he had any messages for me. He said "Yes she's coming soon." I said who and he said "That special woman for you." I smiled.

I was glad my inner child was happy and more positive. This has made me feel so much better, the healing is working. I feel that I've so much to do and achieve in life, that this is the beginning, overcoming my past, my childhood, my fears, and my worries. This will move me forwards; I am me George, I've got so much to give.

## Monday 2/3/98

My inner child appeared wearing his black blazer, smiling, open. He's about fourteen to fifteen. At first he was older about eighteen to nineteen wearing a black Fred Perry tee-shirt, and black stay press trousers just like I used to wear when I was a mod.

I told him he was welcome, and I was glad to see him again. He knew he was safe and that I'll look after him and love him.

He came and sat on my lap, he said he felt better, and I said good. You see this place is special, no-one can come here, only you and I. He said but why does he feel so lonely still? I said because he's got to learn to love himself, believe in himself, and most important to have faith. Faith in himself and faith that he is being looked after; he is special, so very special.

I told him that feeling lonely doesn't mean that you have to feel sad. Loneliness is a time to reflect, to get to know yourself and to love yourself. How could you be lonely if you have a friend within you?

He said why is life bad to me? I said because through it you will grow and become so much stronger, so much wiser. Forget the past, let the fear, the hurt, the hate go, then you will move forward, you will find love in your heart. He told me before he went that strength was within me. I said and within you too, always remember that.

Loneliness is a word that has haunted me for so long. Having something to cling to, to hold to, made me feel safe. I always felt that I needed others to be able to survive; now

I'm beginning to find that I can never truly be lonely when I have a true friend within me. I feel love and compassion I feel within me, the time for self pity is over. I have spent too many years feeling the poor me, I have grieved long enough. Now I must move forward, now I'm never alone, I have my guardian, my spirits around me, how can I ever be alone when I am a part of the universe and it's a part of me?

## Tuesday 3/3/98

My inner child appeared thirteen to fourteen wearing his black blazer and smiling. He was very open and said he was glad to be back, he felt happy here. I said that was good, that he knew this is where he would always be safe and wanted and loved.

He came over to me and sat on my lap. He asked why does he have to be bullied. I said "Bullied at school?" and he replied only at school he was being bullied. I said you are being bullied because they are jealous of you, they know you are better than them and are jealous that's all. I told him that these people will grow up to be bad people, unhappy and sad, and that he would grow up to be strong and better than them. He said "Life's a bully too", and I replied that life isn't easy — you have to go through things before you can grow and be wiser and stronger. But to remember that you are strong and you can face anything, you've faced a lot so far and yet you're here, this isn't the end. I could see that he was happy to be with me in the garden. But I knew deep down he was scared and frightened, he felt vulnerable. He felt that life was the intimidator, and being bullied didn't help. I had to make him feel strong and positive.

I asked if he had any message for me before he left, he just smiled and faded away.

I wasn't too sure if I got through to my inner child, that feeling of being intimidated has lived with me for a long time. I still dream at times of being in helpless situations where I am vulnerable. Do people look at me and see a person capable of looking after himself, or am I still in a way vulnerable? Do I show it, is that why I feel people walk over me, that I'm easily led at times? I needed to get through to my inner child that he will be strong and never feel vulnerable again, I hope I have done this.

At times I have wished that I could go through life without having to rely on others, but that doesn't seem to be the case. Is that why I'm reluctant to let go of the past? I need to be my own pillar of strength, I keep telling my inner child that, but I need to tell that to myself too. I must and will face life and all it has to throw at me.

### Wednesday 4/3/98

My inner child appeared about fourteen to fifteen, wearing his black blazer and smiling happily. He said he was happy, that he knows he is safe and welcome and wanted.

He came over and sat by me, I asked him what information he needed, what I could do for him. He said he liked being at Yaya's (my Nan's) house. That he felt safe there, away from the trouble. I asked him if he got on with his brothers and sisters, and he said "We are always fighting and arguing, just like mum and dad."

I said "How do you feel?" He said he felt different, different from everyone else. I said "Why?" and he said he didn't know, just that he does. He feels on his own, just him, locked away inside his head, that no one understands him, or knows what he is feeling. I said I knew exactly how he was feeling. I told him that he is normal, that everyone feels different, that he could be anyone or do anything, because deep inside him he is strong and positive and can accomplish anything. I told him that his mind was strong, his soul was good and he should not let his emotions overtake the way he feels. That his emotions take him over and make him feel sad and unloved, but that's not the case. He was George, strong, happy and loved. I gave him a hug and wished I could make all his fears, his hurt, his pains go away.

I asked him if he had a message for me and he said yes "Open up your mind and the light will come."

Isn't it strange I'm there to heal my inner child, I know his every thought and yet he knows mine too? He knows that now I'm hurting and he's giving me guidance.

That feeling of being different is so true, different maybe because of feeling that no one really knows you, knows the real George, the George locked away in his cocoon. I was never good at dealing with problems, they always got the better of me, and I'd make them worse than they were. My inner child's feelings and mine are the same, both afraid of having to deal with reality. I remember being fourteen to fifteen when all I looked forward to was sleep. The place I could go to, get away from everything, the place where I was safe. I never wanted to wake up and I tried as hard as I could to not wake up. Now my inner child has the secret garden to escape to, where is this secret garden in reality? I'd like to be there forever.

## Thursday 5/3/98

As I walked over to the fountain, there was white lace and small fairies flying and flowing around it.

When I looked over to my chair, there was a full size fairy sitting in it, a white outline glowing with her crown and wand. As I walked over she got up and flew into the air. As I sat down I looked up and saw her disappear. My inner child appeared fourteen to fifteen wearing his black blazer. He was smiling, open and looked happy. He came over and sat by me. He said "You're here to look after me and love me, I know. I'm safe here and I feel happy."

My inner child told me he wanted to play football, so we did. I asked him what I could do for him, how I could help him. He said he was feeling more confident, happy and good in himself and I said that was great. I picked him up and said to him "We are one, we are strong, we are positive, we are happy. What are we?" and he repeated what I said "We are one, we are strong, we are positive, we are happy." I threw him up in the air and caught him feeling so good, he was smiling.

He said he really liked coming here, and I said "Remember I'll always be there for you always. You are the most important person in my life and always will be, because we are one." He smiled. When it was time for him to leave, he said to me "I am you and you are me," then he shouted "Goodbye, see you soon." and faded away. I shouted back to him "Yes, take care of yourself."

I wish I could spend more time with my inner child, but I'm glad I am able to be there for him. From seeing him being unhappy, sad, to being happy and more positive. Just seeing him smile puts a smile on my face and a warm glow around my heart.

Deep within is my inner child, with him are my love and compassion and my healing. It's true that the power to heal comes from within, I'm glad and happy to have found you to show me how. We all need guidance along our journey and I know that I was meant to meet you. Thank you for giving me the help to meet my inner child, and to begin to heal myself.

## Thursday 12/3/1998

My inner child appeared seventeen to eighteen, wearing a black top and black trousers. He was smiling. Then he turned back to the fourteen- to fifteen-year-old wearing a black blazer, smiling, open and happy.

As I approached the fountain I looked up and saw it was in the shape of the Virgin Mary, with hands out to the side, and a white glow above her head. I stopped and stared. At the base was the fountain with fish swimming around and a variety of colours criss-crossing below the surface of the water.

My inner child came over to me and said hello, he was glad to be back. I asked him how he was and he said he was happy, more positive and had made new friends. I said that was great, see, didn't I tell you that you are special and people do like you. He said that it had been a while since I last came to the garden and I said yes I had to let you get on with being positive and to begin to feel happy with yourself, and I'm glad you have.

I asked him how he was getting on with his brothers and sisters, and he said better than before, but we still argue. I replied that you love them don't you, and he said he did. I told him to have patience with them as they have to learn to grow too, and that he must have more time and love for them. I told him that as they see him become more positive so they will, and everyone will get on much better. I asked him about his mum and he said she's not happy, so I said "Don't you see that by seeing that you're happy she will be too. George you have too much love in your heart, enough for everyone and as you begin to love yourself more and be happy with yourself, so others will be happy too." I asked him how he felt about his stepdad and he said, "Angry, I hate him, it's all his fault." I told him that he mustn't hate, hate is negative and will hold him back. I told him to feel sorry for his stepdad, because it's his stepdad who is weak, and that one day he will tower way above his stepdad and his stepdad will wish he was him.

I told him that he has changed, no longer is he the sad, lonely, negative child I had first met, he was a new happier, better George, because he believed in himself. I told him that I was so proud of him, he will grow up to become a wise and clever person, who does not let hate rule his life. A person who has love for everyone and everything, his reward will be happiness. He smiled, I hugged him and I felt the energy flow between us, as if we had melted into one. I closed my eyes and felt true love, true happiness.

When my inner child was leaving I asked him if he had any message for me and he said "Yes, thank you" and I said I should be thanking him for being there for me too, he smiled and disappeared.

I had not been to my secret garden for a week now and I so much wanted to every day but I knew I had to wait. I have felt like a new person since meeting my inner child, the last week has let me reflect on my life and on me, how I feel, the love that I've found within me. My inner child is becoming the person I wished I was at his age, and now I look back at my past, my childhood and know that it can no longer hold me back. After all that has happened, I've got through it, I am a good person, my strength comes from within.

## Saturday 14/3/1998

Again the fountain was in the shape of the Virgin Mary, with her arms out as if welcoming me into her arms, and a golden glow above her head.

My inner child appeared seventeen to eighteen, wearing his black Fred Perry top and black stay press trousers, his hair was cropped and he was smiling, open and his eyes sparkled.

I welcomed him and said to him that he has grown and that he looked so well. He said "Thank you" and I told him he was safe and that I was there for him. He came over and sat on the arm of my chair. I asked him how he was doing and he said great. He told me that he had a job, he was a trainee domestic appliance engineer and he feels independent. He has more friends and feels so much more happy and confident. I smiled and said "Look at all those doubts you once felt, now look at yourself." I told him that I never lost faith in him and I knew that he could do anything he wanted to. Then I told him I was proud of him and he smiled.

I asked him how things were at home and he said they were getting better but he's out most of the time now. He goes to parties, is with friends and he finally feels he has some freedom. I could see that he was growing up now, doing what teenagers do and I felt that he was so much happier than I was at that age, he was me and I was him.

We went for a walk on the grass and I said to him "Do you remember what I once said to you?" And he said "You mean, we are one, we are positive, we are happy," then he said "Yes I remember." I said "The more I see you, the more we become one." He looked at me and we both smiled and I said "We are one."

While we were walking a thought came over my mind: will he ever want to bring his children to this secret garden? I don't know why I thought this, but then I said to myself "No, his children will be happy and well and looked after. My inner child will always have the secret garden within him and he will pass his wisdom to his children." I felt as if I were Peter Pan, I was that child.

When my inner child was leaving I asked him if he had a message for me and he said "Forever at peace", then he smiled and disappeared into the mist.

I wonder, will there ever be a day when I go into my secret garden and my inner child will not appear? For now I see him as I wish him to be, full of life, happy, positive and not letting life drag him down. I guess I'll have to always say that one day he will move on, his healing has taken him to better things. When that happens I should be happy and not sad, after all we are one.

## Monday 16/3/1998

As I approached the fountain I looked up to see it was in the shape of the Virgin Mary, with hands out to the side, and a glow above her head.

My inner child appeared about seventeen to eighteen, smiling, happy and open. He was wearing his black Fred Perry top and black stay press trousers. He said that he had been mixing with a lot of people and that he was in a gang. He didn't like all of the people he was mixing with but he had to fit in. He said some of them take drugs and that he tried some speed. I told him that all teenagers want to experiment, take drugs, smoke, but taking drugs was wrong. Taking drugs is only a way to escape from problems, escape from reality. Drugs were not a substitute for having fun, fun is when you are in control and have all your senses about you. Then I told him that he was better than his friends, he didn't need to take drugs. He smiled, then said "I know you're right but I like smoking, everyone does it." I said "I have been there too and my friends have died from drugs, some are junkies now." I told him that smoking is a bad habit, but he should think to himself that he is better and deserves better things out of life. He told me that he did, that he just wanted to be happy and have fun. I said "You will, and you will attract the right friends around you because you are a good person." Then I told him I would always be there for him and that he can tell me anything. I told him that I will not judge him but I will give him good advice and guidance, just like he does to me.

When he was leaving I asked him if he had a message for me and he said "Happiness awaits you."

My youth was all gangs, drugs, drink, cigarettes, and seemed so exciting. So many times I put myself in danger, so many times I got into situations that I wished I wasn't in but I always kept my wits about me, or so I thought. I took drugs, sniffed glue and then found I was easily led and got into more trouble. But one day I realized that I was better than that and I walked away from it all. I don't know if that took courage or what, but losing my friends was hard for me. But were they really my true friends? That is what my inner child must understand. Life can easily suck you in, but I know he'll do the right thing.

## Wednesday 18/3/1998

Again the fountain was in the shape of the Virgin Mary with her arms out as if welcoming me into her arms, and a golden glow above her head.

My inner child appeared seventeen to eighteen, wearing a red Fred Perry top and blue trousers, he was smiling, happy and open.

I said that he was welcome and that he was safe and wanted. He smiled. I asked him to come over and sit by me and he did.

I told him that he looked well and happy and that I was happy to see him. He said he was fine, things were beginning to fall into place. Then he said to me "Is there a God?" I said "Yes, you know that, but why do you ask?" My inner child said that for a long time he had prayed that everything would be OK, that deep down inside he felt something, but yet his troubles had still gone on. I said to him "George, you are a very deep person, that is because you are spiritually very aware. For you to find yourself and the love within you, you have to face certain things in your life, and it is different for everyone." Then I said "How can you ever say that you know life when you haven't experienced the pain, the happiness, the joys and the troubles that come with it?" He replied OK, but why has he always felt different, that someone was watching over him? I said that the same person who watches over him watches over me too. Then I said "I know what you mean by saying you feel different, that is because you are changing, you are developing into a better person, and as you do so you will attract other people like minded to yourself."

I told him that God is in everyone and everything, that he must love everyone and everything and never let hatred, anger and fear take over his life. I told him that love is the most powerful tool that we have, for those that have hurt you, pass on thoughts of love to them, they can never hurt you again. I told him that there are many religions and beliefs in the world which is OK. They all believe in someone or something and at the end of the day it's all the same, it's the divine light that leads us. Then I told him that one day he will see and feel it, then nothing will ever truly hurt him again.

Then I told him that he should not feel that because others are not like him that they are no good. It is just that they have yet to go where he is in life and that it is good to ask questions, but he should always follow his heart. I knew he understood and he smiled at me.

When he left I said goodbye and he said "There is a bright light around you" and he left.

At a time when I am finding my spirituality, my inner child asks if there is a God, and I knew what he meant when he said he felt different. I knew how he prayed at night, how he used to look at the icons and shrines at his Nan's house and how he would pray. He would pray to not hurt any more, pray for happiness, stand in awe in the Greek Orthodox Church looking up at the paintings covering the walls and the ceilings. How he wished an angel would come down and take him away. I knew all this, and yet as I grew older I let life take over and lost sight of what I once wished for. It never came true so I lost faith. One day I will be sitting somewhere talking to my own children and they will probably ask me the same question "Is there a God?" and I will say "Yes, you are living proof of the love of God."

*Rita's Story*
Rita, a lady in her mid-50s, presented with phobias and chronic low self-esteem, one symptom of which was her complete lack of confidence in social situations. In her childhood her mother had ignored her to the point of not cooking meals for Rita unless

the father also was home. Her brother was a sadist and would beat her up (he later enjoyed a career as a mercenary). Home life for little Rita was so bad that she preferred to stay at the hospital where she had several operations. When it was time to leave the hospital she would hide under her bed, and then again under other children's beds once her previous hiding place had been discovered. Rita was sent away to a Convent boarding school where the nuns were sadistic in the execution of their responsibilities. She later married a man she did not love so that she could have a family that she could feel she belonged to.

*Rita's Inner Child Diary*

## Monday 10/3/08

My inner child appeared immediately after I had asked her to show herself, she was twelve to eighteen months old and was withdrawn. She was wearing a white dress, white ankle socks and black patent leather shoes. I sat on the grass beside her, asked her if she would like to sit on my lap, which she did. Again she did not want to talk; her only need seemed to be physical comfort. I stood up and carried her around the garden. She had her head on my shoulder, her body pressed to mine. The more I walked around the garden, the more she began to relax, although she still had no interest in talking.

When it was time to leave, I simply put her on the ground and she walked away.

I could associate with my inner child; I also enjoyed the comfort of being held closely, conversation was unimportant for now, there would be sufficient time in the future to talk.

## Tuesday 11/3/08

I arrived at the secret garden just in time to see my inner child enter the garden, smiling, open, and looking quite happy. She was wearing the same white dress, white ankle socks and black patent leather shoes from the day before. Again she was aged twelve to eighteen months. She walked straight over to me and I picked her up and asked if there was anything she would like to tell me. She said she was happy to have a friend and I told her I would be the best friend she could ever have. I would always be there for her, she could talk to me at any time, come to me for comfort whenever she liked. She did not have to wait until she felt sad before coming to me, I would be happy to talk to her, hold her and love her all the time.

I walked around the garden holding her close; again there was no need for further conversation.

This time when it was time for me to leave I could sense she was reluctant to go, however she did walk away quite happily.

I was very tempted to keep her with me especially as she was reluctant to leave, however home life is not very comfortable at the moment and I would prefer a more harmonious atmosphere for my inner child.

## Wednesday 12/3/08

I entered the secret garden and noticed the comfortable chair had changed from the chair I used as a young child into a chair I usually use now. My inner child was standing beside the fountain aged about two, wearing a blue and white dress, white ankle socks and white sandals. She was very excited and open. I asked if there was anything I could do for her and she replied that I already had just by holding her and giving her comfort. I told her that she had helped me also and that we were obviously gaining comfort from each other.

We walked around the garden, watching the butterflies flitting from one flower to another. It was a special time for both of us, holding each other, growing closer and closer.

I asked my inner child what her needs were and she replied that she needed to feel loved. I told her that I would always love her very, very much. She then asked why no-one else loved her, to which I replied that I believed her sister loved her but more importantly I was capable of loving her more than anyone else, my love would be all-encompassing, helping her to feel safe and secure.

When it was time to leave the garden I asked my inner child if she had a last message for me. At first she said she didn't then she changed her mind and looking very shy asked if I was certain I would always be able to love her. I asked what she meant by always be able to love her, I didn't understand. She said she did not feel worthy of unconditional love. Again I assured her that I would love her under any circumstances. She appeared unsure of my answer but smiled and walked away.

At first I was uncomfortable discussing my feelings, having spent most of my life suppressing feelings and emotions. However, I soon relaxed and felt very emotional towards my inner child. When I told her I would always love her I really did mean I would always love her.

## Thursday 13/3/08

As I looked around the garden searching for my inner child I saw her sitting on the wall of the fountain. She was five years old wearing a white top, yellow shorts, white ankle socks and white plimsolls on her feet. She was open and appeared to be serious but happy. Her hair had been cut short, which obviously did not please her as she was pulling it downwards, as though trying to stretch it to cover more of her neck.

I picked her up and placed her on my lap, at the same time asking if I could do anything for her. She replied that she was quite comfortable at the moment but would like to ask some questions later, after she had had a nap. She said she was tired but would feel safe sleeping on my lap. I rocked back and forwards as I would rock a baby and within a few moments she was asleep. She awoke after what appeared to be only a few seconds, stretched, then stroked my face. I asked what questions she would like to ask and she replied that there were many questions to be asked, many answers to be given, and didn't know where to start. I told her I would answer all the questions to the best of my ability and to begin at the beginning and work through them all. She then asked why she always felt lonely, I answered she felt lonely because she had no friends, but now I was her friend and I would be the best friend she could ever have, I would always be there for her to talk to, to be close to, to keep her company, and in general just be there for her. She then asked why people hurt her, again I told her I would protect her, I would not let anyone hurt her, and that all the hurt she felt was now in the past. She had a future to look forward to, she would be happy and secure.

She appeared happy with the answers to those questions, so I asked if she had any more questions for me and she said she was still tired and could she ask more questions the next time I came to see her. I told her she could and that I would hold her until she fell asleep, then leave until tomorrow when I saw her next.

This conversation with my inner child has made me feel a lot lighter in myself. My concerns about loneliness and being hurt are shared, no longer such intense feelings of sadness. I am looking forward to meeting my inner child again tomorrow, healing the past, sharing my sadness, and for once believing there may be a reasonable future.

### Friday 14/3/08

I entered the secret garden longing to see my inner child once again; however, she kept me waiting some time. When she did arrive she was aged seven, very closed and unhappy. She was wearing a blue and white mohair jumper which itched terribly, a white skirt, white ankle socks and blue shoes.

I told her that I was very pleased to see her and she replied that she had not wanted to come today, she did not want to see anyone. I asked why, but before she replied I knew the answers. I understood how she felt and also knew she would not want to talk today. I picked her up and held her silently. She put her arms around me and I could feel her misery.

When it was time to leave I didn't ask if she would like to stay with me, I knew she needed to be alone, as I also needed time to think.

Age seven was the most difficult year of my entire life. So many things happened during that year. I felt like becoming bitter with people, society, everything, railing against anyone and anything, becoming an anti-social delinquent. Luckily, I realized that would be false to the real me. I may like to be defiant, uncaring, cruel even; however, I had to accept I was too weak to stand up for myself, too frightened of the pain to come. By this time I had developed a high physical pain threshold (or could "switch off" quite easily), however, emotional pain was more than I could endure. This year was by far the worst year of my life; however, I am too hurt, embarrassed, ashamed and humiliated to accept the situation, although thankfully I am not able to be angry. I don't believe I will ever be able to accept verbally or emotionally the events of this year. Sorry, I really do want to change my life around — need to become a survivor, and in a lot of ways this is happening. I am more confident and assertive, which is fantastic; however, this year leaves a great impression on me. In this year, I had the final operation on my neck, the first operation on my arm, the year I realized that there was no hope of my mother even acknowledging my existence, the year I began to change schools regularly, the year I listened to my father's cruel comments. I learned not to cry or show any emotion, the year pain became a friend (something I could feel), "switching off" to physical pain no longer gave comfort, life was a roundabout of suffering, anxiety, fear, denial, lost hope and total devastation. I feel a need to become a survivor, not a victim, and honestly this is going in the right direction, but I have spent a lifetime being completely closed in all aspects of life, and try as I might, I find being open is very difficult. When in hypnosis, I understand my feelings, but when I return to full consciousness I can't explain, or I can't explain how being closed is hurting too much to talk. Neither can I explain how some things can (you have the experience to disagree with me) cut so deeply that even when in hypnosis I am very frightened to acknowledge some situations.

### Saturday 15/3/08

My inner child appeared aged ten, wearing a white blouse, navy blue skirt, white ankle socks and black shoes. Her hair had grown quite long and it was tied back in a pony tail. She was open and appeared quite happy.

I asked if I could do anything to help her feel better and she said she felt OK but maybe I could help her inner child! I looked to where she was looking and saw a seven-year-old girl looking very sad, sitting on the grass with her head in her hands. This child was my inner child, and so was the ten-year-old my inner child. The seven-year-old still had short hair, which didn't please her, she wanted to be accepted and believed her appearance was important.

When I asked the seven-year-old inner child if I could do anything to help her feel better, the ten-year-old inner child sat beside her and held her hand. I sat beside them both, facing them, placing my left hand on the leg of the seven-year-old and my right hand on the leg of the ten-year-old. The younger inner child replied that she wanted to leave home, never return, and never be hurt any more. I told her she needed to have courage for now but the time would come when she would leave home, would never be made to return, and would never be hurt to the same extent as she was hurting now. At seven she had already learned more about life than the majority of adults and all these experiences would benefit her in the future. Her understanding of cruelty, her compassion to others, would in many ways help her to help others. I told her I would remain close to her at all times, and I would love her unconditionally and help her to grow big and strong. I would protect her from others, I would be strong for her, I would not let anyone hurt her physically or emotionally.

As I was leaving I asked if she had any last message for me and she said that she felt better knowing she could rely on me to protect her. I told her that she had nothing to fear any more.

That was weird — a young inner child comforted by an older inner child. My father would have accused me of schizophrenia!

### Sunday 16/3/08

My inner child appeared, aged eight wearing the green blazer, white shirt, tie and grey skirt of G.... High School.

She was uncomfortable but not unhappy. I asked what I could do to make her happy, she replied she was not unhappy, just resigned to life the way it was at the moment. When I asked what life was like at the moment, she replied it was not too bad, her brother and sister were both at university, her mother had a lovely woman working for her and she enjoyed her company. Her father was returning home most nights now — he was preparing himself for semi-retirement and took work a lot easier.

I then asked if she needed anything from me, and she replied that she needed only what other children take for granted: comfort, safety, and hope for the future. I asked if she would like to sit on my lap, which she did, and then I told her that I would always be there to comfort her, she could come to me at any time that she felt she needed comfort. I would protect her at all times, I would not let anyone or anything hurt her, and her future would be as she wished it to be. Whatever she chose to do, she could achieve.

Again as I was leaving I asked if she had any last message for me, and she replied that she was looking forward to my next visit. I told her that I was looking forward to seeing her again too.

I can feel a difference in myself as though my care for an inner child is healing the adult. This is definitely very powerful material.

Having spent a great deal of time in hospital, I soon realized that my family life was not what could be termed typical, and in this case ignorance would definitely have been preferable.

## Monday 17/3/08

My inner child appeared aged eleven to twelve, wearing black trousers, white jumper, and black shoes. She was open and appeared to be very serious.

I asked my inner child if there was anything she would like to tell me. She replied that she was unsure how life would change when her father retired. He was very lazy and would expect everything to be done for him. He also had a terrible temper and could be violent when provoked. At the same time, if her brother came home during the holidays, then she would be safe. Her father would protect her from her brother, although it was going to be a difficult situation. I suggested that she should wait and see what transpired. Safety from her brother was a great thing, something that she had wanted for many years. Her father did care about her, and the attention she received from him would probably outweigh the occasional outburst of temper. The main issue was not to provoke him in any way and to always remain quiet and unobtrusive.

We walked around the garden, taking a path we hadn't noticed before, and came across a small stream. My inner child asked if we could take our shoes off and walk in the stream. I said I thought that was a great idea, and we walked and splashed in the stream for some time.

When it was time to leave I asked if she had a last message for me. She said she hoped I had enjoyed splashing in the stream, and I told her it was great fun, and I looked forward to doing it again. Before my inner child turned to leave the garden, she said she would try to keep her head down when her father retired. I replied that she was doing the right thing, in time everything would change, and that she just needed to be strong for now. I told her I would be there to help and advise her at all times, and that between us everything should be OK.

I remember being concerned when my father mentioned retiring early, mostly because of the work load that would be passed to me. I certainly did not mind working hard, but I didn't think I was physically capable of doing more. My mother employed a woman to do most of the housework, but the remainder was usually left to me. My father expected everything to be perfect which could create a difficult situation.

## Tuesday 18/3/08

As I waited for my inner child to appear, I walked to the fountain and looked inside at the water and the fish swimming around. The goldfish were of different sizes and different shades of gold all swimming in the same direction as though racing each other.

Today my inner child was again aged eleven to twelve and was open and very happy. She was wearing a blue gingham dress, blue blazer, white ankle socks and black shoes. Her hair was tied in bunches which made her appear young and mischievous.

Again I asked my inner child if there was anything I could do to help her, and she replied that she would like to change some white flowers into different coloured flowers. I agreed, so we spent some time collecting white carnations and white asters. We collected water from the stream and found some food colouring on the grass. The carnations started to change from white to blue and white, and others to red and white. The asters started changing to dark blue, pale blue, red and pink. To finish we started to change a white aster where one half was blue and the other half was red. I suggested to my inner child that she could continue watching the changes take place until the next time I would see her. She thought this was a great idea as the changes were very gradual.

All too soon it was time to leave my inner child. This time, when I asked if she had any last message, she told me that she had had a lovely day. She didn't know how to play and really wasn't interested in playing, she would much rather learn about all things, anything really as long as she was learning.

I am finding I am able to relax with my inner child; in fact I am very comfortable with her. Daily I look forward to meeting my inner child, we know each other so well, understand each other, and love each other.

## Wednesday 19/3/08

When my inner child appeared she was aged nine and very frightened. She was wearing a pale blue top, dark blue skirt, white ankle socks, and blue sandals.

I asked why she was so frightened and she told me her brother would shortly be home from university for the summer holidays and her parents were going on a cruise to Norway. I reminded her that her sister would also be home from university at the same time and that she would protect her. I also told her that nothing should frighten her because I would be there to help her, protect her, take care of her and make sure that she would be safe. Anne was quite capable of occupying John and would see that he had many other interesting activities to occupy him. Mother and father would only be away for three weeks which would pass quickly. My inner child was not convinced; she knew, and I knew, we could not change the future. We held each other without speaking, words could not be spoken by either of us.

When it was time to leave I asked my inner child if she would like to stay with me; she was delighted, saying then she would feel safe. I have taken her with me and shall take great care of her.

While my parents were on this cruise my brother broke my nose.

I will arrange to take tomorrow off work and take my inner child to an open air museum. As a child I would dream about going to museums, castles, the Roman Wall, or in fact anywhere historical. I would also have loved to go to a circus and/or a pantomime, however this is not the pantomime season, and I don't think there are any circuses in the area at the moment.

## Thursday 20/3/08

We woke up early (5.00 a.m.) and we were showered and dressed by 5.45 a.m. After a leisurely cup of tea (I have only drunk water for many years), we decided to have porridge for breakfast. When I produced soya milk from the fridge my inner child pulled a face and looked quite disgusted. I asked her not to judge until she had tried it, which she reluctantly agreed to do. Once it was made and she tried porridge made with soya milk she did admit it was very creamy and nice. Next we woke the boys, saw that they were washed and dressed, made their breakfast, and prepared them a packed lunch for school. Once everyone was ready, it was time to wake Amy and then take the boys to school. I checked in at the shop before my inner child and I headed to the museum. This is the first time I wished I had not sold my car. Taxis are OK but too restricting when not 100% sure of the outcome of the day. Once we arrived at the museum we looked at the displays with great interest. I did not have to explain anything because my inner child understood as much as I did. In fact she laughed at me because a lot of what was in the museum I could remember from my childhood. I think I aged very quickly within a very short period of time! Next we went to the museum farm where there were ducks, geese, hens, goats, pigs, a few cows, a bull and horses. Again, having lived in the country, we were used to seeing these animals, although there were quite a large variety of different breeds of hens.

Soon it was time to leave, having seen all there was to see, so I suggested we could go to a country pub for lunch. This was something my inner child was excited about, so we walked into the village and found an old quaint pub. The menu was plain but the atmosphere was great. There was an open fire and old but comfortable tables and chairs. I asked my inner child what she would like to eat and she chose cheese omelette and chips. I did suggest something healthier, but then gave way and ordered cheese omelette and chips and a glass of lemonade which she thoroughly enjoyed.

Eventually it was time to collect the boys from school and head home. My eldest grandson mentioned that I looked happier than I have for a long time. If I had told him why, I think he would try to have me sectioned — he is such a serious boy.

It is now 9.00 p.m. My inner child and myself are exhausted so shall be going to bed soon. This has been one of the best days of my life. My inner child has been fantastic company; maybe I did get a few strange looks, grinning like a Cheshire cat when to all appearances I was by myself. I look forward to many more days with my inner child, now or at some time in the future.

## Friday 21/3/08

My inner child is still with me and we are enjoying the company of each other, we understand each other, know what the other one is feeling and thinking. We are totally compatible in all ways.

Today, I have arranged to take all four of my grandchildren to the park. It is a lovely park with a boating lake, pets' corner, playground and many playing fields. I am sure my inner child will enjoy the park and will also enjoy the company of my two eldest grandchildren who are very serious, as is my inner child.

We have a wonderful day playing on the swings, throwing a ball around, eating ice cream and candy floss. All the children would have loved to go on the boats, unfortunately as a non-swimmer this was impossible (I would not let them go themselves), although all four children can swim reasonably well.

Once again my eldest grandson notices a difference in me, and comments that I have been more fun to be with than usual. Maybe a grandmother behaving like a nine-year-old is not such a bad thing.

When the day is over, I ask my inner child if she misses the secret garden, and she replies that she has had great fun but, yes, she does miss the secret garden. I am relieved because I know Saturday, Sunday and Monday would not be very good days for her to remain with me. She would not be happy as I know I will not be happy, and I do wish to protect her in all ways. She suggests that she could return to the garden and I could continue to visit her there until the next time she felt the need to stay with me. I agreed but asked her to grow away from being nine years old and suggested aged ten or over would be best for her. She replied that she had grown up a lot during the last two days and now knew how much I loved her and cared about her.

## Saturday 22/3/08

My inner child appeared aged fourteen, very serious, yet appeared serene. She was wearing the Convent uniform, i.e. brown skirt, brown and white shirt, and a ridiculous brown bow tie and equally ridiculous brown waistcoat.

I said I was very pleased to see her and would she like to sit beside me. She sat next to me on the comfortable chair and asked if I had any strength I could pass on to her. I answered that she herself was strong, stronger than she believed, however she could still take strength from me. I would give her all the strength she needed, now and in the future. We stood up and walked towards the fountain in silence, and then I asked if there was anything she would like to tell me. She replied that I knew all there was to know, that she was not too unhappy for herself but felt a great need to protect those more vulnerable than herself. However, she was not in a position to do more than occasionally give comfort. She was well aware if the nuns learned that she tried to comfort those suffering at that time, then she would be expelled. Two Spanish sisters had been expelled for comforting each other after the death of their much loved grandmother.

We returned to the comfortable chair which had again changed and was now the chair in my bedroom at the convent. Neither my inner child nor I sat on the chair.

When leaving I asked my inner child if she had a last message for me, and she replied that she felt bitter towards nuns in general, which was a shame.

I think my inner child must have been feeling very generous in her explanation of how she feels about nuns. I find it very difficult to be polite to nuns, instead I would like to ask what right do they have to inflict pain and suffering on to young children, all in the name of God? This convent may have been strict to the extent of cruelty, however, I was very lucky not to have been with Nazareth House where unforgivable cruelty was inflicted upon those in their care as late as the 1990s.

### Sunday 23/3/08

My inner child appeared aged fifteen and was open and happy. She was once again wearing the convent uniform. She walked straight over to me and I stood up and put my arms around her. We held each other for some time then we walked towards the path that led to the stream. Without any words spoken, we removed our shoes and walked into the stream. I laughed and then my inner child laughed with me.

I asked if there was anything I could do to help her, and she replied that she had been doing a lot to help herself. When I asked what she had been doing, she told me that she had been teaching herself shorthand and touch-typing and was doing quite well. With luck, by the time she reached sixteen she would be quite proficient and would be able to leave the convent and home behind her. If she could find employment and somewhere to live she would be very happy. I told her that she would be able to achieve this, that her life would be difficult at first but she would be happy. Earning very little as a sixteen-year-old, paying rent and bills, would be extremely harsh but achievable if she budgeted well. I told her she was capable of achieving anything she desired if she worked to this end.

We walked to a grassy area, dried our feet and put our shoes back on. We were both very happy and behaving like five-year-olds, laughing and generally being silly.

When leaving I asked if she had a last message for me, and she told me to stop being so serious and that life can be fun. I smiled and she turned and walked away, waving her hand and laughing.

I did leave school at sixteen, taking a job in a solicitor's office as an office junior, and within six months I was promoted to secretary to the senior partner. The hard work

I endured learning shorthand, touch typing and basic book-keeping certainly proved advantageous, especially as I pushed myself to the limits to achieve exceptionally high speeds. I managed to afford a bedsit as soon as I was promoted, and so left home aged sixteen years six months. I was very happy for the first time in my life, mainly because my employer was a wonderful man, and was also the first person I knew I could trust.

## Monday 24/3/08

When my inner child appeared she was aged eleven to twelve, very open and happy. She was wearing a navy blue and white track suit and white tennis shoes.

I asked my inner child if she had anything to tell me and she said she had just played in her first tennis match and had won. She hoped to be accepted on the team but would have to wait and see. I told her that if she wanted to play on the tennis team then she would succeed, that she was capable of doing anything that she wished. She told me she enjoyed playing tennis, it was something that she felt she was good at, and she could lose herself in the game. Again I emphasized that she could be good at anything she tried, providing she wished to be and worked hard towards this.

We walked around the garden, hand in hand, appreciating the delicious smell of the various flowers. My inner child told me she felt very lucky to have someone who could understand her so well, knew her in all ways possible, and would love her unconditionally. I told her that I also felt very lucky to have her, and that we understood each other in every aspect of life, and were capable of loving each other at all times.

When leaving the secret garden I asked my inner child if she had a last message for me, and she replied that she felt happy and secure. I told her to hold onto that memory, to keep the memory close to her heart, and always remember just how lucky she is. She said she would do that, and always feel happy and lucky. We waved to each other then she turned away from me and skipped into the distance. Just before she faded into the distance she turned around and waved again, she was smiling and looked very happy.

It was lovely to see my inner child looking and feeling so happy. I believe this is a reflection of my own feelings as I am happier and more content within myself than I have been for many years. There are changes to make and I now know I will make these changes.

## Tuesday 25/3/08

My inner child appeared aged thirteen to fourteen, and appeared to be open and happy. She was once again wearing the convent uniform.

I asked my inner child if there was anything I could do for her, and she replied there was nothing that she needed, she was feeling quite happy, although a little apprehensive. When I asked what was making her feel apprehensive, she explained that she would be going home during the holidays for the first time since she had arrived at the convent and wasn't sure what to expect. She said she didn't know whether Anne and John would be home. She had heard that John had married but wasn't sure if that was correct. Anne had written to her some time ago and told her that he was getting married, although she had not heard if indeed he did marry. I explained that John could never hurt her again, whether or not he would be at home. She was no longer a young child and his power had now ceased to exist, she could no longer be intimidated, frightened or humiliated by him. He was weak and she had gained strength as she grew older, his only strength had been in abusing a child. She need not fear anything as I would also be there to protect and care for her.

Once again we walked around the garden, this time we walked along the path leading to the stream only to find the stream had become a lake with swans and ducks swimming on the surface. We threw bread onto the lake for the swans and ducks to eat and we laughed to each other as they fought one another for the largest morsel of food.

As I was leaving the secret garden I once again asked my inner child if she had any last message, and she replied that she believed she could see a brilliant future for us both. I replied that I hoped she was right and we could spend many more happy times together.

My brother had married and by this time had a son. I very rarely met my brother from this time on, although his friend and my brother would intimidate, humiliate and embarrass me whenever we did meet. Whenever my parents were aware of the situation (often in their presence), they would consider it to be quite amusing. After the birth of my son I refused to acknowledge the fact that I had a brother and would not allow myself or my children to be in his company under any circumstances.

## Wednesday 26/3/08

I walked towards the comfortable chair and noticed it had again changed into the chair I used when I was a child. As I waited for my inner child to appear, the chair seemed to grow as though to accommodate a larger child. My inner child did appear aged fifteen to sixteen and seemed confident and happy. She was wearing the convent uniform once again, although this time she was also wearing make-up, albeit very faint.

My inner child came straight to me and sat down beside me on the now larger chair. She told me that she was very happy to see me and was looking forward to the future. I told her that I had missed her since the last time we had spoken and was very pleased to hear she was looking forward to the future. She replied that she would very soon be making her own way in life, she would leave the convent at the earliest opportunity, and felt quite sure she would be employed in a menial role very quickly. If she were not allowed to return home at the present time, then she would worry about where to stay when the need arose. I wished her luck and expressed my belief in all she could and would achieve. She had been trying to contact her sister in the hope that she may be able to stay with her, although she had heard nothing from her for some time and her father would not mention her in any correspondence.

I asked my inner child if there was anything I could do for her, and she replied that at this moment she was happy and had all that she needed. She had a future to look forward to and could allow herself to hope for a better life. I wished her luck for her future and advised her to take care of herself and to remember I would always be there for her in any way she wished. She thanked me and told me we would always be there for each other at all times. I agreed we have become united in every aspect of life.

When it was time to leave the secret garden I asked my inner child if she had a last message for me and she replied that we would be together always in mind, body and spirit. I agreed we will always be part of each other.

My sister was disowned by our parents when she became pregnant aged twenty-five and did not marry the baby's father — he was already married. Anne and Tom lived together with the baby. Tom in turn was disowned by his family when he eventually obtained a divorce and married my sister (Tom was a Jew), and in the way of most dysfunctional families, my parents accepted my sister back into the fold once their grandson was no longer classed as a bastard. They were extremely happy together until Tom died when their son was approximately eight years old.

### Thursday 27/3/08

My inner child appeared aged sixteen, very open and very happy. Again she is wearing the convent uniform and a small amount of make-up.

I asked if there is any information she would like to give me, and she replies that she is looking forward to leaving the convent very soon, she has saved enough money for the train fare home, although she does wish she had the courage to go anywhere else but home; she would like to start afresh somewhere new. She is confident about finding employment. Tony had already told her on her last visit home that there would be a job waiting for her, so if she went elsewhere she may end up out of work and homeless. I empathize with her, I know exactly how she is feeling, to move away from all that can or has hurt is very appealing, although not exactly what could be termed as secure or safe.

We walk to the fountain and watch the fish swim around. This time they are swimming in all directions, looking confused, very much as we feel. As I am preparing to leave the secret garden I ask my inner child if she has a last message for me, and she tells me to look and find a future that will give me pleasure. I promise I will, if possible, and she tells me to forget about "if possible" and just do it!

Wow! I didn't expect that! It is very much a case of second time around. I am not happy with my life now and have often thought of moving to a different area, starting a new beginning, although I lack the confidence to make a complete break. Always concerned about where I would live, how I could support myself, would I select a safe environment, etc. Maybe I should play the *Confidence Booster* more and listen to my inner child more!

# Tuesday 1/4/08

My inner child appeared aged sixteen, open and happy. She was wearing a multi-coloured cheesecloth skirt and top, flowery beads, and had bare feet. Her hair was dyed red and was worn in long plaits.

I asked my inner child if she would like to sit beside me on the grass, which she very happily agreed to do. Once she has settled she takes hold of my hand and asks if she can do anything to help me. I reply that I am OK, and I should be asking her the same question. She laughs and tells me she has become quite mischievous lately, not unkindly mischievous, purely creating a lighter atmosphere, trying to create joviality in others. I agreed helping others to feel good and enjoy life is a great achievement, and I wished her luck with her progressive outlook. Again my inner child chastises me and advised me to "lighten up and enjoy life", to which I laugh and agree to accept my own advice.

We once again walk around the garden and I notice my inner child appears sprightlier, more relaxed, as though having been relieved of a heavy burden. When questioned she replies she is feeling content, she is working quite hard and enjoying her work, although it is a bit tedious, but at least she is making progress and in time she will make more of a career for herself. She is happy and is in a situation where she can and will learn a great deal which will please her as she has always been anxious to learn as much as possible in most contexts.

When the time arrives for me to leave the secret garden I ask my inner child if she has a last message for me, and she replies that the time has come for me to lighten up and not be so serious. I laugh and ask who is helping who? She replies that we are helping each other; we have no alternative as we are the same person, becoming more in tune with each other.

Did I really wear those clothes? Yes, when I think about it, I wore "hippy clothes" until I was approximately thirty.

My inner child was very happy, mischievous and content with life slightly earlier than I anticipated. At this time I was living at home and had believed I only became happy with life after I left home a few months later.

### Thursday 3/4/08

I walk around the garden looking for my inner child, and then find her making daisy chains beside the fountain. She is aged sixteen years and six months, extremely happy and open, wearing a navy blue suit, white shirt and navy blue shoes. Her previously dyed red hair is now quite short and dyed a more sedate shade of brown.

When I reach my inner child I sit on the grass beside her as she puts the daisy chain around her head and announces that she will now have to curtail her more outlandish hippy appearance as she has now become Tony's secretary and would be mixing with clients quite frequently. I agreed that she would be required to be slightly more sedate with her attire, but I hoped this would not inhibit her exuberant spirit now that she was expressing herself, openly, verbally and physically for the first time. She smiled and asked me to take a good look at her hair, clothes and feet and then check her out later when she has had time to change out of her work clothes.

We continued making daisy chains which my inner child wrapped around her wrists and ankles until it was time for me to leave. As I was leaving I again asked if she had a message for me, to which she replied that she did not today, other than she looked forward to seeing me again soon. I told her that I also looked forward to seeing her soon.

This was definitely a time of two people living in one body. I would leave for work as a hippy, and then change in the toilets at work, emerging as a typical business woman, dignified and formal. In personality, a carefree adolescent would evolve into a studious, capable and official appearing individual. It was great fun as I could be a carefree child enjoying music and clothes, and five minutes later become a mature and responsible personality discussing probate and conveyancing. During business lunches with Tony he would often comment that he would prefer advanced warning as he never knew where to eat, the local "chippy" or somewhere "posh".

### Saturday 5/4/08

My inner child appeared aged seventeen and was extremely happy and open. She was wearing a navy blue skirt, white shirt and navy blue shoes.

I asked my inner child if there was anything she would like to tell me, and she said she was happy, happier than she could ever remember. She saw her sister occasionally but didn't bother with the other members of her family, not that they were interested in her life now any more than they had been in the past. I told her that it was only important that she was happy, she need not be concerned with anyone else. She had Anne, Tom and her nephew, and of course Tony and myself to care about her. There were more people now to care about her than there had ever been, and of course she knew she could always rely on my being there for her at all times, now and in the future.

We walked along the path that leads to the stream which we have enjoyed on other occasions. When I next looked at my inner child she had changed into "hippy" attire once again, looking very mischievous with bare feet and cheesecloth clothes. Before I could speak she jumped into the stream, splashing me, laughing, and calling for me to join her, which I did. We splashed each other for some time before again drying our feet on the grass. Once again as I was leaving I asked my inner child if she had a last message for me, and this time she told me to splash around or at least try a little mischief, just once, it may be fun!

At that time in my life I don't think I realized just how lucky I was. There were people in my life who I respected, although I was only able to trust Tony. Unfortunately, most of the memories I had of my sister were lost, along with some very unpleasant memories, only to be uncovered many years later. I feel as though I have done her an injustice now, not realizing that she did all she could in extremely difficult circumstances.

## Monday 7/4/08

My inner child appeared aged seventeen to eighteen, open, although she appears to be serious. She was wearing a flowing multi-coloured skirt, a beige loose top and Jesus sandals. Her hair had returned to its original blonde colour and was tied in quite short bunches.

I asked my inner child if I could help her with anything as she appeared to be quite serious. She replied that she had been asked, by Tony, to take the exam to become a legal executive. He had taught her all she knew in probate and conveyancing, and believed she would do very well. However, she was not too sure; every time she was in an examination situation she panicked and would forget even the most mundane information. Also, she had been very successful working as a legal secretary and yet had no formal qualifications, so believed she could continue helping with probate and conveyancing without formal qualifications. She did not under any circumstances enjoy doing matrimonial or criminal law. Matrimonial law felt like an invasion of privacy, and she could not enjoy criminal law when children murder children. I suggested she should do as she thought best. No-one else knew fully how she felt or how much she would or would not enjoy being a legal executive.

I didn't take the exam, it was not important enough for me, and when I talked seriously to Tony and explained that I would much rather be extremely good at the work I was doing than be mediocre at something that was more advanced, he agreed, especially as it was beneficial to him for me to remain with probate and conveyancing. If I had taken and passed the exam it would be necessary, especially at first, to incorporate all aspects of law into my workload.

## Thursday 10/4/08

My inner child appeared aged seventeen to eighteen looking open and happy. She was wearing a white mini skirt, white jumper and white boots. I asked my inner child if there was anything she would like to tell me, and she replied that life was improving day by day. She enjoyed work very much, often working late into the evening. She had no friends, no social life, however she did not feel as though she was missing anything. Work was her solace; now that she had a key to the office she was no longer lonely, she enjoyed the work and thrived on the responsibility.

We walked to the fountain and watched the goldfish swim around in all directions. Each fish appeared different either in size or markings, some pale gold with black markings, others bright gold with white markings.

When the time came to leave the garden I again asked my inner child if she had a last message for me. She replied that she looked forward to seeing me again, to which I answered I would miss her and was very proud of her.

I found this session very difficult to visualize, at times, and feel that the time I spend with my inner child is coming to an end. The healing is nearly complete, for which I shall be eternally grateful. I would never in a million years believe I could be so much more confident, which is great. The difference in me is noticeable to many, including friends and family, even customers who have accused me of using "happy baccy".

*Postscript*

Rita described her Inner Child experiences as "weird". When I asked her what she meant by "weird", she commented: "It's gone against my analytical mind." She said she now felt "a lot more content, happier with myself... I don't feel alone." Interestingly enough, in a later session dedicated to her fears of being above ground level (including on a step ladder which her work required) or in open spaces, her subconscious recalled that she had attempted to end her miserable life at the age of twenty by walking over a cliff — something you would think a client would remember to mention to her therapist when discussing fear of heights! She obviously had not consciously recalled this event, but its recollection along with another incident where she was knocked unconscious off a step ladder at the age of five (and no doctor was called by her parents!), were reframed successfully so that their phobic effects were dissipated. The remaining phobia resolved itself as if it had never been there, and Rita did not look back from enjoying a more confident social life. Unfortunately, although she managed to outlive the prediction of her doctors by eighteen months, Rita finally succumbed to cancer in 2011.

It's worth reminding you that this inner child therapy has the effect of "rewriting history". Rita mentioned on occasion being surprised how confident her inner child appeared from times in her life that she otherwise remembered as miserable.

This is because of all the loving and healing that occurs in these meetings. As I've said before, most people were happier at the age of 5 than at 15, but the inner child over time will tend to come through older and happier, which is the opposite of what your memory will tell you. To repeat myself, this *Meet and Heal your Inner Child* process is like taking a time machine back to a moment of need, and plugging that emotional hole, fulfilling that need. That's why it's powerful stuff!

Reading Rita's inner child diary, you will see that Rita sometimes took her inner child with her. If you meet an inner child who would be quite upset for you to leave at the end of your time together, and *only if this becomes a regular feature* in your meetings, then take your inner child with you. To do this, make your inner child really small and put her/him in your heart. However, you must now give your inner child your full attention! In my opinion, it is much better to leave your inner child in the beautiful secret garden where she or he is safe and secure, but missing you a little, than to take her/ him with you only for you to ignore her/him; especially if you have been promising your inner child that you will always be there for her/him!

In this case, talk to your inner child; give your inner child treats, maybe some chocolate or an ice cream; share your food, music, books and games with her/him; or take in the fragrance of flowers, the beauty of nature — spend good quality time with your inner self.

As you listen regularly to this session and love and heal your inner child, she or he becomes older and happier, and you yourself come to feel that you are truly worthy of love from others, and can be secure and happy in your relationships, and now deserving of what Life and the world have to offer you.

When you have reached your target of twenty-four diary entries, and can feel the difference in your everyday levels of self-esteem, then you are ready to progress further with the *Supreme Performance and Self-Esteem Booster* session.

### A note for survivors of sexual abuse

Although this "It's Never too Late to Have a Happy Childhood!" inner child therapy is appropriate for survivors of abuse, it sometimes happens for a few of my clients that the abused child is reluctant to appear when they have listened to the *Meet and Heal your Inner Child* session. This is despite the client knowing or remembering that they were sexually abused. It could be that she or he is still hurting even after their adult self has promised to protect them.

If you have a similar experience, then I strongly recommend that you seek out a therapist who is proficient in Soul Retrieval therapy, which is the next scheduled session after meeting their inner child for clients of mine who have suffered trauma or sexual abuse. The soul retrieval sessions that I have been fortunate enough to facilitate have been truly remarkable to witness, and utterly transformational for the participants. They go on a journey into a dimension of spirit guides and power animals to retrieve their lost parts or fragments, "kick the ass" of the perpetrators, and re-integrate their parts so that they can be truly whole again, and be able now to move forward in their life with all their power. Links to more information about this powerful therapy and approved practitioners can be found in the *Resources* section at the end of Part One **Human Doing**.

# CHAPTER TEN
## *The Supreme Performance and Self-Esteem Booster*

The *Supreme Performance and Self-Esteem Booster* session goes further than the initial *Confidence Booster* session because it addresses the three most common and specific situations in which people feel most intimidated or nervous. It also deals with negative self-beliefs, allowing you to reprogram yourself for greater confidence in personal, social, professional and formal situations. Because this session is such an advance on the *Confidence Booster* session, it now makes that session redundant — unless you have some emotional attachment to the *Confidence Booster* session, you won't need to listen to it any more.

After a short progressive relaxation induction, I will take you down the ten steps to a gently sloping hillside overlooking a lake. Again, it's important that you imagine this place rather than using a memory of an actual hillside or lake. Summer is the season I have chosen as that is the most popular. Once you are relaxed in that place, the therapy starts.

You will be presented with a list of negative adjectives, names, criticisms which others may have called you since childhood, at home or at school; and even words that you yourself may have used in the past to describe yourself. Once you have deleted those negative labels, you will have an opportunity to rewrite the list, so please do so using the opposites of those negatives, as well as all the good qualities that you want for yourself. I will suggest a few to get the ball rolling, including CONFIDENT and ARTICULATE. There should be enough time for you to write your own positives, and for you to focus on and absorb them, before we go into the "Supreme Performance" and visualization part of the session. "Visualization," as I tell my clients and students, "is all about giving your subconscious a blueprint of the desired behaviour." So when you hear me suggesting that you can speak confidently to *people in authority, to groups of people, and to new acquaintances,* and that they will be respecting and admiring you, it is important that you tailor this session to your own circumstances and requirements, and that, first of all, you have examples of each of those three categories that apply to you; and secondly, that you visualize any upcoming events or "tests".

*People in authority* can include bosses, interviewers, decision-makers; police, teachers, medical doctors and consultants, government officials; and anyone else who intimidates you, perhaps relatives or fellow workers with overpowering personalities.

*Groups of people* applies to both informal and formal situations, from being in the company of friends to leading major presentations; from family gatherings to being in front of a panel of decision-makers.

*New acquaintances* means meeting people for the first time. This could apply to all new acquaintances, male and female, but for some it also applies to meeting people to whom they are sexually attracted. If this is the case for you, then that is the scenario you should visualize, especially if you are going out with the intent of meeting a potential partner. So when you hear me say *new acquaintances*, in your mind you could add *including men/women you find attractive*, as well as imagining that scenario going well.

Go to www.humandoingandhumanbeing.com to access the *Supreme Performance and Self-Esteem Booster* session. Once again, please use headphones.

## After listening for the first time

I hope you enjoyed relaxing on the hillside. How many negative labels were there? The average is six to eight, so you are doing well if you had less than six, but there's still some way to go if you had more than eight.

Just to clarify, you never need to add anything to the list of negatives, you just glance at and deal with what's there. So if, for example, you have been called *clumsy* since childhood, you may find that *clumsy* is on the list the first few times you listen to this session, and so you delete it and replace it with, say, GRACEFUL, AGILE or ELEGANT. One day you may be listening to the session and you look at the negatives to see that *clumsy* is no longer there — this is as it should be, your negatives get less and less. However, we all have good days and bad days. One day you might drop your papers, spill your drink, or bump into someone or something, and when you next listen to this session *clumsy* may well have returned for a short time. But please accept that regular listening to this *Supreme Performance and Self-Esteem Booster* session will reduce negative labels, self-beliefs, programming and conditioning, while at the same time increasing your belief in yourself and your confidence in your abilities to perform in the world.

A visualization check now. Were you able to see yourself performing really well in those three scenarios (and any others you may have added) of interacting with people in authority, groups of people and new acquaintances, and that they were respecting you and admiring you? If for any reason you didn't, then make sure you do so when you next listen to this session!

Until you find no negatives, I recommend listening to the *Supreme Performance and Self-Esteem Booster* session ten times before progressing to the final *Your Goals* session for Part One **Human Doing**. As a matter of interest, there is a little-known technique that can easily be used in situations where you might feel nervous or anxious, and as this forms one of the spiritual truths in Part Two **Human Being**, I have chosen to talk about it there at the end of Chapter Three.

For those clients who have been healing their childhood with the *Meet and Heal your Inner Child* session, I would now be recommending a Time Line Realignment session after the *Supreme Performance and Self-Esteem Booster* session and before the final *Your Goals* session. Time Line Realignment, or TLR, is my own patented therapy process which is ideal for those of us who may be stuck in the past, i.e. find it difficult to move on from incidents or trauma in the past, including loss and the end of relationships, or for those who cannot envisage a positive future, e.g. depressives. As TLR relies on the client's feedback to the facilitator, it has not been possible for me to include it here. For any of you who choose to work one-to-one with one of the therapists trained by me, enjoy your TLR journey! A North American acquaintance of mine once addressed a group of students in Manchester some thirty years ago. I remember to this day his dry laconic sense of humour and his slow drawl as he delivered this pearl of wisdom regarding being "stuck in a rut": *What's a rut? A rut is a grave with the ends kicked out.* TLR is ideal for those who are "stuck in a rut" as it enables them to put the past behind them, be in the present, see that there is a future, and that it's a positive future, and that it is attainable!

At this point, I would like to advise any therapists who are interested in using these self-development sessions one-to-one with their own clients to please undertake the professional training that is available. Please do not jeopardize the therapy of your clients by assuming that everything you need to know is in the pages of this book. Clients should check that therapists they are considering working with have the appropriate certification and accreditations, as well as full indemnity malpractice insurance.

## CHAPTER ELEVEN
# Attaining Your Goals

By this stage, if you have followed my recommendations and listened to the previous audio self-development sessions the required number of times, you should be feeling much more in control of your life situation — more confident, more resilient and optimistic in the face of challenges, and more positive about what the future holds for you. All that remains to do now is just some "fine-tuning" with the *Your Goals* session.

Just imagine for a moment now what your life could be like if you had absolute confidence in your own abilities to meet any and every challenge, and to succeed with ease. The *Your Goals* audio self-development session enables you to banish any remaining negative inner voices and to enjoy happiness in your personal life as well as success in your worldly life.

After a short relaxation, I will take you down the ten steps to a path that leads you through the woods on a bright sunny day. As this session focuses on your goals, please have some goals ready! Take a few moments now to think about

137

what you really want to get out of life: your hopes, dreams and aspirations; and which achievements would mean a lot to you. Goals for some people are tangible, by which I mean material and external; for others they are intangible, e.g. internal. For example, "Success" for the former might mean a mansion, limousine and helicopter landing pad, whereas for the latter it might equate to having the esteem and respect of his or her colleagues — the latter person would visualize himself or herself feeling this when I ask them to see their goals. "Happiness" for some people might be visualized as an attractive partner in life with two or three happy healthy children, whereas for others their happiness, which might include partner and kids, would be visualized as themselves enjoying the feeling of happiness that comes from having that. So please have some goals ready for you to visualize in the session.

Then I will ask you to remember some past goals, and these could be academic or athletic, as well as professional. Why do I ask you to recall past successes? Simply to give you the confidence to take the first steps toward your new goals, to remind yourself that you have been in that situation before — perhaps not on such a grand scale — and that you succeeded then, and you can succeed again now. I will then ask you to make a conscious decision to let go of any form of Self-Doubt, Pessimism (as in "It works for everybody else, but why should it work for me?") and Procrastination (as in having good ideas but never getting round to implementing them). Once you have made those affirmations to yourself,

I will then paint a picture of how your life can be without these sabotaging programs.

Go to www.humandoingandhumanbeing.com to access the *Your Goals* session.

## After listening for the first time

I hope you were able to see yourself and your goals in life, as well as any past successes or achievements, and that it was easy for you to let go of the remnants of any negative programming from the past.

Please listen to the *Your Goals* session regularly over the next four weeks to keep on track. Feel free to alternate with any of the other sessions you feel you need. In the *Resources* section that follows, I advise you about which future situations and circumstances it would benefit you to listen to the most relevant specific sessions again. But for now, I want to congratulate you on having taken this journey of self-improvement, and I sincerely hope that you have experienced many positive changes in your confidence, attitude and expectations of life.

I hope you will join me in Part Two where we will explore your spiritual nature, the true purpose of your very existence, and the opportunities that are available to you to discover and experience this birthright for yourself.

## CHAPTER TWELVE

# *Resources*

Once you have completed the program of self-development outlined in **Human Doing**, you now have available to you a "tool-box" of resources that you can utilize again in the future. I can give you some idea of when you might want to revisit your sessions by describing possible future scenarios where the use of each one would benefit you again. For ease of use I have listed all of them here, whether or not your personal program as prescribed by the Self-Esteem Tests included all five.

### Session 1: *The Confidence Booster*

Although Session 4 the *Supreme Performance and Self-Esteem Booster* session has probably rendered this session redundant, there may be occasions when you need extra confidence in one-off daring or challenging situations, e.g. a charity parachute or bungee jump. If this is the case, listen to the Confidence Booster and visualize it going well when you hear the words *You are able to do everything you want to do.*

## Session 2: *The Multi-Level De-Stressor*

This is the session you should remember to use in the "down times", i.e. at times of great stress, or when your emotions could be said to be "all over the place" — at times of illness, death of loved ones, relationship worries and perceived setbacks. Listening to the *Multi-Level De-Stressor* enables you to process the emotions and get through that down time more quickly.

## Session 4: *The Supreme Performance and Self-Esteem Booster*

It's good to listen to this session from time to time as part of a healthy maintenance program, and especially if and when you have a very important meeting coming up, e.g. auditions, job or promotion interviews (performance or salary reviews), Best Man's speech, large-scale presentations, that crucial date, performances to audiences on stage or in public, etc. Positive visualization by you of these upcoming events is essential when listening to this session.

## Session 5: *Your Goals*

Perhaps in a few years from now, when you have reached all of today's long-term goals, you could listen to this session again and visualize your next set of goals.

## Session 3: *Meet and Heal your Inner Child*

If you are feeling vulnerable for no particular reason, then that may mean that your inner child requires your attention or help; especially so if you still feel like this after having first listened to the *Multi-Level De-Stressor* session and/or already attempted to "let it go in real time". You may need to listen to the *Meet and Heal your Inner Child* session more than once until she or he is happy and the telltale signal of vulnerability is no longer felt.

## My websites

For more about this book and the author OR as a good starting place to link to the other sites listed

*www.CostaLambrias.com* or *www.CostaLambrias.co.uk*

For one-to-one clients

*www.holistic-hypnotherapist.co.uk* and
*www.selfesteemdoctor.co.uk*

For hypnotherapy training and the Academy of Holistic Hypnotherapy

*www.ahh-hypnotherapytraining.co.uk*

For training in Soul Retrieval, Past Life and Inner Child therapies, Time Line Realignment, *Human Doing & Human Being* and *"First Be, then Do"* Consciousness workshops, etc.

*www.soulconcern.co.uk*

## Other recommended websites

SleepTalk is The Self-Esteem Program for Children (and their parents). Ideal for three- to twelve-year-olds, SleepTalk instils confidence and resilience, and creates a harmonious dynamic in the family unit

*www.sleeptalkchildren.com*

You can write me with your personal accounts of how your life is changing with the self-development exercises and audio sessions

*costa@selfesteemdoctor.co.uk*

I am also on Facebook and Twitter.

If you have really enjoyed your experiences as a result of going through the self-development sessions, then please spread the word and tell others about this book so that they too can benefit. A special "Thank You!" from me if you can spare the time to leave a review on Amazon that would help others who might be considering purchasing this self-help guide.

# PART TWO

# Human Being

*"Who or What you are is not a name, job title or relationship — it's a consciousness and a feeling. That feeling is Love. First Be, then Do."*
(Costa Lambrias)

# CHAPTER ONE

# Being versus Doing

*"Happiness resides not in possessions and not in gold, the feeling of happiness dwells in the soul."*
(Democritus, Greek philosopher, 460–370 BC)

*"The way forward for you right now requires no movement or action, rather it is a remembrance of your true divine nature. First Be, then Do!"* (Costa Lambrias)

I SINCERELY HOPE THAT YOU have reached this page having experienced in just a few weeks the benefits of the **Human Doing** self-development exercises and audio sessions in Part One; and that, as a result of undergoing these proven processes, you are indeed experiencing greater confidence in all your interactions with others, and that life for you is a more positive experience on so many levels. You may now be enjoying improvements in your relationships, in your career prospects and, most importantly, in how you feel about yourself.

And now that you are experiencing a greater sense of self-worth, it would be easy to stop reading and coast along with the occasional "top up" of the appropriate self-development session in order to maintain your progress in the world, and that is just fine. However, I am guessing that many of the people who invested in this book did so for reasons of spiritual self-development, so I invite you to read on! And for those of you who have never asked those questions about the purpose of life, but have enjoyed the journey through Part One so far, and are curious about what the author means by *Human Being,* then please keep an open mind and an open heart as I extend that same invitation to you too to discover more about "your true purpose", and how to experience THE reality that lies beyond time, space and mind, and yet is closer to you than a heartbeat.

To begin, I would like to prepare you for Part Two by putting some context to Part One and explaining some of the major differences between Part One *Human Doing* and Part Two *Human Being*.

In Part One where "unconscious" referred to the subconscious mind, here in Part Two it is most likely to refer to a lack of spiritual awareness; so "conscious" now means "spiritually aware" when before it meant "awake, thinking", as opposed to being in a trance or altered state of consciousness. Some of the differences are as follows, with Part One (Doing) listed first, versus Part Two (Being):

### Doing vs Being

Concerning worldly matters — your place in the world (material expectations, success and prosperity) vs Concerning your spirituality — your place in Creation (Being, not Doing)

Unconscious (governed by the mind and ego) vs Conscious (aware of your true nature)

Mental and emotional health and well-being vs Spiritual well-being

So-called Psychotherapy (mind) vs True psychotherapy (soul)

Self-therapy vs Self-realization

Mundane, worldly and materialistic vs Magical, mystical and spiritual

Achievement / success vs Surrender / enlightenment

Attachment (pain) vs Detachment (spiritual perspective)

A reality that appears real, i.e. Illusion vs THE Reality, Truth (Perceived reality vs Actual reality)

Identification with the mind vs Beyond body and mind — your true essence

The Power of the subconscious vs The Power of Nothing (no thing)

The Importance of good self-esteem vs Who / What Are You?

De-programming / re-programming and healing vs Experiencing the Oneness

External vs Internal

"Hell" vs "Heaven"

Somewhere vs Nowhere / Everywhere

Existing ("empty, unfulfilled") vs Living ("complete, fulfilled")

Space and Time (limited) vs Infinite and unlimited

Descartes ("I think, therefore I am.") vs Jung ("Who looks outside, dreams; who looks inside, awakes.")

Mind vs Heart / Soul

I will also be talking about Energy, vibration and frequency, and the nature of the True Reality. To illustrate further the difference between Human Doing and Human Being, I reproduce below my diagram from a short article published in the UK in 1996 on *The Role of Consciousness in Therapy.*

HIGH = COSMIC / SPIRIT

"BEING"          ONENESS          LIGHT
(less to do... "doing" nothing?)

FREEDOM          FULFILMENT          CLARITY

CONSCIOUSNESS = VIBRATION / FREQUENCY OF ENERGY

RESTRICTION / LIMITATION          NEED / LACK          CONFUSION

(more to do)
"DOING"          SEPARATION          IGNORANCE

LOW = EARTH-BOUND / PHYSICAL ("UNCONSCIOUSNESS")

*Costa's Diagram: Consciousness as the Vibration / Frequency of Energy*

This diagram is biased in favour of Consciousness. What I mean to say is that an "unconscious" or low-consciousness person may very well not be aware that he or she is "separate" or confused and that his or her life lacks anything at all. That is because until now these people have not had experiences in life or internal feelings that have caused them to question the very purpose of their own and mankind's existence. Their reality is that of the physical and mental. They identify themselves as their mind and their body; they do not know, or even suspect, that each human being is much more than this.

*All of the problems of this planet can be attributed to a lack of consciousness, i.e. a lack of our true spiritual awareness.* It is because the majority of human beings are identified with their mind and their ego that they see themselves as separate from all other humans. People are divided because of their disconnection from the real and available experience of that which gives life to all Life. Because of this disconnection, they experience it as separateness; not being able to connect with "it" (the source, the essence of all) means that they do what all "lost souls" do — they identify with their mind and their ego, and they are unable to accept or envision a higher, spiritual perspective to everything that happens in their life. This separation leads to an "us and them" mentality; "them" can be different sports teams, countries, ideologies, political factions, religions, etc. These symptoms of disparity and disunity manifest as terrible wars and the deaths of millions of fellow earth dwellers. As the Buddha says: *"This world is only a mirror of your consciousness."*

For real, positive and lasting change that will bring an end to hunger, war, environmental chaos, cruelty to and death of other species as well our own, all that is needed (!) is a shift in Consciousness. For a change in Consciousness, *every human being needs to become conscious.* In other words, you need to rediscover your true essence, thereby fulfilling your potential and your birthright as a Human *Being*, not a Human *Doing*. You do this primarily for yourself, not for the planet, but in so doing, others can benefit from your increase in consciousness. My mission in Part Two of this Evolutionary Guide is to facilitate your success in achieving the inner purpose to your life.

## CHAPTER TWO

# *Who / What Are You?*

*"A drop melting into the ocean, everyone can see.
But only a rare one can see the entire ocean absorbed
in a drop!"* (Saint Kabir, 15th Century Indian mystic)

*"You are not a drop in the ocean.
You are the entire ocean in a drop."*
(Rumi, 13th Century Persian mystic poet)

Y OU HAVE A BODY, and yes it's a physical body. As amazing a creation or object as that is, I believe most of us can agree that we think of ourselves as not just a body; in other words, that the body is something we inhabit, a carrier or vessel for who we really "are". The person called Joe identifies himself as something more than his body. He can tell you that he is intelligent, has a personality, and possesses a good or poor imagination, all of which have very little, if anything at all, to do with his body. If we think about friends or loved ones, they may have certain physical attributes that we find attractive, but most of us would agree that what makes them unique or special (i.e. "what makes Joe Joe") is something that has nothing to do with their physicality. And most people would call this *Mind* rather than *Soul*.

Mind effectively runs the world. Your own mind controls you, and collective Mind controls the world. We invest everything in mind, we trust it, we believe it, and it has succeeded in leading us up a blind alley. Why do I say this? Because your identification with your mind as your self, to the exclusion of all other possibilities, keeps you a prisoner, bound by your beliefs and concepts, and ignorant of the reality of what exactly *it* is that is maintaining your life at this very moment and every other moment, as well as the continuing existence of the rest of material creation.

It's not your mind that sustains Life, and gifts you this and the next breath. It's not your body either, yet without *it* your body and brain would shut down in an instant. Once this "energy" is gone, so are you.

By now, you may be one of the many who believe I am talking about *Soul*. I am, and I'm not, so please read on.

*"The only thing that interferes with my learning is my education."* (Albert Einstein)

"Home is where the heart is." What does that mean? For some people, they take it to mean that whatever they are fond of doing, or wherever their loved ones are, is where they should be. I am here to tell you literally that your true home in this universe is not an external construction but can be found at a point inside your body which is the source of Love. To get to that point you go beyond your thoughts, you connect with it inside yourself, and it vibrates with pure love — it's the love that the creator has for its most-loved creation, you! You were already connected to *it* when you were born, and most people witnessing a birth or a sleeping baby get to sense that; it's a comfortable and almost familiar feeling that acts as a reminder to our soul for us to reconnect.

But then what happens after birth as a matter of course in this world is that we get "educated" by our parents, teachers, Society and Religion. I find it both ironic and humorous that it is because of a grammar school education that I am able to tell you that "educated" means "led out of" or "led away from" (from the Latin *ducare*, to lead or raise; and *e*, short for *ex*, out of or away from). And so the journey of disconnection begins! We lose that simple natural connection to the source and sustainer of all matter, our connection to the Oneness, as we are given names, identities, aspirations, expectations to fulfil, desires, career paths, goals, etc. All our attention has now been shifted from the pure and simple feeling that is inside to an outside world that is physically and mentally real and that demands all of our attention now — literally, we have now gone from within to without! Our senses maintain this outside focus as our mind convinces us that the sensations and feelings that we really want to experience *inside* us now have their origins *outside!* Ironically, everything we do in the world, every new sensation we seek, and every meaningful relationship we have, is to find that experience that we came from and to which we must return. The trick is to experience it now, or as various spiritual teachers exhort us, to "Die before you die." I personally prefer to say to "Live before you die!" as without our connection to the source, we are like sleepwalkers who cannot awaken.

*"Through Love, the dead will all become alive."* (Rumi)

Your mind, that you cherish so much and with which you identify yourself so completely, is *The Biggest Thief.* It deprives you of experiencing your true state of being: the Truth, the essence of all matter, the Divine. It does this because there is no room for it in the true reality, and so it continually deludes you into believing that what is important is You along with everything you have to do to survive, succeed and "make it" in this world, in Society. This is not the real you, the "you" from which you came and to which you return when the body dies — and that you can reconnect with and "be" at any moment! — but the other you, the egoic you that you and others have nurtured throughout your life. That you has been so real for so long, and now I am shaking you gently but firmly to wake you up from this dream.

This world seems real, and yes, when you identify only with the dimensions of Time and Form, you lose the connection to the Timeless, the essence of every particle, the Love inside and behind all of creation, and which is manifest most abundantly in you — not the dolphins or the stars, but you — hence your title "the crown of creation".

And through all this time that we are unaware of our true essence, and ignorant or forgetful of the opportunity that each moment gives us to reconnect, *it* still keeps us alive; *it* is patient, loving, and waiting for us to reconnect and join in with its dance of the heart. For many, that doesn't happen again until the time of death, death of the mind and body, a time when your soul can rediscover its true essence.

I am talking about something that is beyond mind, body and soul. Despite many so-called spiritual practices, especially in the East, that involve the abuse or punishment of the Truth-seeker's or God-seeker's physical form, the body is such a precious thing because it is the container for your life essence, and therefore it is the bridge between the finite and the infinite. As such we must value it and take great care of it. The mind is supposed to be a tool that can help with — rather than create — problems or adverse life situations. We are supposed to use the mind, but the truth is that we are so subservient to it, that the mind is constantly guiding and controlling us and making sure it has all our attention, so that we never get to reconnect with what was there before it had control of us, and what is in fact always there in the background even while we are engaged with the mind. I am hoping to "educate you in reverse" — to show you how to step away from the mind so that you may experience the true reality.

We are made up of mind, body, soul and Spirit.

Emotions can cross mind, body and soul. The mind thinks, and thoughts often can turn into emotions or restimulate past emotions; emotions can be felt in the body and by the soul. Soul is You, your personality, your uniqueness (the "what makes Joe Joe") that sets you apart from all other souls and beings. Spirit is the *it* I have been referring to. Nothing exists without it. I repeat, it is inside everything, sustains and maintains everything, and there is nothing that exists that doesn't have Spirit as its essence. It is the vibration, the primordial frequency, of the whole of creation, and *you have inside your physical body your own portal to its omnipresence where its attribute of the purest love can be felt by you.* And when you feel it, you feel it vibrating in every atom and molecule; you are no longer aware of your physicality, your "outer shell", you are one with it and the rest of the creation. To get to that portal you need to go beyond thoughts, to sit still, and be still. Lao Tzu, the father of Taoism and author of the Tao Te Ching, expressed this truth so: *"To the mind that is still, the whole universe surrenders."*

*"Look at you, you madman! Screaming you are thirsty and dying in a desert, when all around you there is nothing but water!"* (Kabir)

*"How holy is the stillness for in it is found your heart and your soul's essence — the vibration of Love, of Life, and of the whole of creation. Be still... Be!"* (CL)

*"I think ninety-nine times and find nothing. I stop thinking, swim in silence, and the truth comes to me."* (Albert Einstein)

*"God. Divinity. Truth. Love. Peace. These are not outside of you, they all lie within, behind each and every breath. Just stop Doing and start Being."* (CL)

*"There is a life-force within your soul, seek that life. There is a gem in the mountain of your body, seek that mine. O traveller, if you are in search of That Don't look outside, look inside yourself and seek That.*

*This aloneness is worth more than a thousand lives.*
*This freedom is worth more than all the lands on earth.*
*To be one with the truth for just a moment,*
*Is worth more than the world and life itself."* (Rumi)

*"Inside the almost insignificant drop of this moment*
*lies the ocean of infinity and supreme consciousness.*
*Can you be small enough to fit?"* (CL)

*"If only you knew what bliss I find in being nothing."*
(Rumi)

For you to gain an appreciation of your formless form, and also perhaps a glimpse into your divine nature, I invite you to listen to *A Glimpse*. To access this session please go to the www.humandoingandhumanbeing.com website. I recommend you use headphones in order to maximize your enjoyment of this trip. Close your eyes but keep your heart open to receive.

## After listening for the first time

I hope you were able to gain an appreciation of the value of this human body beyond its physical form; and that "you are not your body" but much more than this. I use a more basic version of this session with clients seeking to release themselves from addictions to substances such as cocaine and heroin. You may choose to repeat this session whenever you feel the need to remind yourself that you are more than what this world would have you believe you are, and also to prepare you for the meditation practice outlined in the following chapter.

*"Impermanence. We are blessed that everything in the world including our physical body is temporary, otherwise why would we seek the divine?"* (CL)

In my early days of spiritual practice, I used to sit and "meditate" twice a day. As I will explain later, there are five distinct aspects to experiencing the presence of the spirit Godhead within you. In order to experience these five tangible attributes — and through each of which you experience your whole being vibrating with the creator's measureless love for you — I would attempt to connect with my heart by turning my attention and my senses from without to within, from outside to inside.

One of the aspects is visual. In those early days I would sit and practise the visual by going inside and opening up to what was inside of me. I found myself traversing galaxies and universes at an incredible speed.

165

I experienced for myself that *everything that is outside is inside*. The whole of creation is interconnected. It is one thing believing that, it is another to have the experience of it. I can tell you though, that for me the experience of that is of absolutely no value or spiritual significance without the overwhelming sensations of stillness, deep deep peace and Love that accompany it! Intellectually, it's good to know that you aren't a tiny insignificant life form rotating on a tiny planet that it is itself less than a speck of dust in one of countless galaxies and universes, etc. ad infinitum (or *ad nauseam* in my case at nineteen, as related in the Preface); but to experience the creator's love at the heart of every bit of matter as you vibrate at the frequency of the divine is a gift, and that love is completely unconditional. Some spiritual teachers would say that you have already achieved the hard part — for whatever reason you are the possessor of a human body which is the vessel for the divine and the gateway / link / portal from the finite to the infinite; and you have an opportunity with every breath, at every heartbeat, to merge with the divine, the supreme God consciousness, and to experience the Oneness.

The closest example I have found to help explain how everything outside is inside is that of the holographic plate which has light shone through it to project a three-dimensional image or hologram. I have been told that if you were to break a holographic plate and hold any fragment up to the light, you would still be able to see an image of the whole, not just a part of the whole. Each one of us is like that holographic fragment, most of our life feeling disconnected and separate from the whole, unconscious and unaware of our true nature and the potential we have to fulfil our life's true purpose.

I want to talk further about "the interconnectedness of all things".

This is a concept that is easily understood and accepted by most people these days, i.e. that "everything is energy." Believing this brings you no closer to God! In fact, such concepts, whether based in science or religion, are loved by the mind because, like every mind-originated concept, they prevent you from experiencing the spiritual truth. *As long as the mind is creating, fantasizing, comparing, understanding, judging, conceptualizing, synthesizing, or fitting the infinite into a nutshell, it prevents your soul from merging with the divine; as long as your mind is active, no matter how noble or "spiritual" your thoughts are, you cannot go beyond the mind!* The words of truth contained in the following chapters, however, have the power to cut through the chatter and interference of your thinking, as their expression of *What Is* resonates with your soul that recognizes the truth of all things.

There is a universe of difference between (A) understanding — and indeed having the experience of — the interconnectedness of all things, and (Z) experiencing the Source of all matter and of all creation. A on its own gets you no closer to Z; however A is a side-effect, a symptom if you will, of Z. It (A) may be useful information to have, or a mind-blowing experience to share with other interested parties, but the latter (Z) cuts across all concepts, beliefs and dimensions as it is the all-of-you-encompassing experience of the Whole, the oneness of everything. To further illustrate the difference between A and Z, I will talk about the Remote Viewing course I attended near Loch Lomond in Scotland in 2007.

Remote Viewing was practised by both US and Soviet military intelligence during the Cold War. It enabled either side to locate the other's secret installations, such as concealed missile silos. The remarkable thing about it was that in the US "ordinary" soldiers were recruited as remote viewers, no degree of psychic ability was required. I believe it was started in the early 1960s, and officially those departments are no longer in service.

The reason I had enrolled on the week-long course in Scotland was because I had "received" information over two sleepless nights while in a dream state, presented to me as if I were watching a film. I was sure I had the framework for a conspiracy thriller involving psychics and others characters with parapsychological abilities which included remote viewing and remote influencing. Soon after, I met with one of my Academy of Holistic Hypnotherapy students who told me about the Remote Viewing course she had attended at Loch Lomond with Mike Webster. I found her experiences fascinating, and in order to properly research remote viewing for my book / film, I signed up for the next one.

I would sit opposite Mike with a table between us. He had a large brown envelope with an A4-sized picture inside. I had a note pad and pencil. In typical military fashion we would designate a code for each "mission", then I would allow the pencil to form a short squiggle, an "ideogram", on the sheet next to the code. I would tap the pencil on the squiggle and open up to receiving information about the subject of the picture inside the envelope, e.g. whether there were "biologicals" (human or animal life forms) there or not. While tapping on the ideogram I would receive sensory and emotional information. Three things became clear: firstly that I wasn't tuning into Mike for the information because whenever I came up with new information about the target site for verification, he would have forgotten what the picture was and would have to look again inside the envelope; secondly, that I had to ignore my mind that wanted to put two and two together and invariably take me "off-line"; and thirdly, that the information I was receiving was coming from the actual location or subject of the picture, and not from the picture in the envelope — in other words, that I was at the target zone, sensing it remotely. This sounds amazing, but at the time it felt perfectly natural.

On Day Two, one of my early assignments brought up the presence of metal, the smell of gunpowder, the sense that it was like a stockade, but that people actually paid to enter this place and enjoyed being there. By the time I'd got all this information, my mind had added it all up and wanted to jump in with "It must be a Wild West show, a reenactment of a gunfight." Mike, and the threatening cudgel he kept in sight at his end of the table, always reminded me to ignore the mind's chatter and to rely on the information I was receiving by other means. I also got a sense of the presence of water at the target. When Mike removed the picture from the envelope it turned out to be an old promotional photograph of Cardiff Castle, probably taken in the 1970s judging by the look of the cars being driven on the road outside. There were gun cannons, but no water to be seen. Even though it was early into the training, I felt absolutely certain that there must be water there, so much so that when I got back to my lodgings that evening, I telephoned my sister who had lived in Cardiff to ask her if the castle had a moat around it that hadn't been evident in the photograph Mike had used. She didn't know. The next day when I arrived back at Mike's, the first thing he did was show me a picture of Cardiff Castle he had taken the previous evening from Google Earth. Sure enough, the moat of water was there.

On Day Five, my final mission was to build out of modelling clay that day's target. I really had to trust the information I was getting, i.e. trust myself, not my mind, especially as some of the info appeared contradictory: big building with a huge arch-shaped entrance, hot outside and bustling with people, while inside in the relative darkness and shade it was cooler, and there was a great sense of reverence; however, despite the huge arch-shaped doorway, it couldn't be Saint Paul's Cathedral in London because I sensed four square turrets and a huge gold dome. I also got a sense (and built as best I could with the clay) of the bustling stalls set out for tourists and souvenir hunters that stretched out to the right of this place of worship. When Mike revealed the photograph I was pleasantly surprised to see how much my clay model resembled it (I'd used white clay for most of the building and orange clay for the golden dome). Also in the photograph was a tourist bus outside, however because the photo was centred on this tourist-destination mosque, it didn't show the traders and their stalls on the roadside, but I swear to you they are there!

Whilst training in remote viewing, I had experienced being in a different location to my body, and being able to sense what was there, as perfectly normal activities. It was only a few weeks later that I realized what a mind-blowing achievement it had been. I had experienced the interconnectedness of all things, BUT I had only experienced it on a mental level. Yes, it had been mind-blowing, but it could hardly be called fulfilling or "spiritual" in the truest sense of the word. I had learnt something that was a pale reflection of the experience of oneness that I feel whenever I go inside. I had "done" (Human Doing) rather than "be". As such, it was dry when compared to experiencing and bathing in the ever-flowing never-ending pool of Love that permeates me, you, and all life. There have been times in my life when I have sat in a quiet room to meditate, not for my usual forty-five to sixty minutes, or even for two hours, but rather I have sat down to merge, to never return, with no schedule, constraints or targets of time, just a thirst to merge, to be One. Those "meditations" were fulfilling, and allowed me to remain in God consciousness long after the formal meditation had physically finished and I had got up to blissfully continue with the other activities and responsibilities of the day.

*"Lift the veil that obscures the heart and there you will find what you are looking for."* (Kabir)

What do I mean by Meditation? I have already expressed that it is about shifting your attention from the outside physical world and focusing within inside of yourself to the love, peace and perfection that is always there and can be felt when the mind is still. *You are in this world, but you are not of this world.* Your true "form" is the formless that is in nothing and everything, nowhere and everywhere. I do not mean to speak in riddles, I am just suggesting that what most people hold to be "real" is matter in a fixed or fixated state, which is just the physical surface of ever-flowing vibration. For us to experience that vibration, and thus attain union with God and enlightenment of the soul, we need to listen out for that pure vibration's frequency so that we can then merge with it, and find ourselves resonating with it (our spirit) and literally every thing. Imagine if you will a divine tuning fork perpetually vibrating at the frequency of Love throughout the universe and all of creation, including inside your soul which is the real Heart inside your body.

In your normal worldly consciousness, you cannot feel the divine tuning fork or hear it. You need to close all your senses to the world and shut the door to your mind. Your mind will fight against it out of self-preservation. It wants to maintain the status quo and its position of control over you. Merging with God consciousness and with that pure vibration may mean death to the mind and to the ego, and so whenever you attempt to shut it up and experience what lies beyond it and within everything, it will do everything in its power to disrupt your experience. It's like attempting to place the record needle onto an LP (long-playing vinyl record) of the harmonious and pitch-perfect sound of the divine tuning fork, and the needle keeps jumping all over the place! What you need to do is to slow down and be still enough to begin to feel your own internal vibration humming at the same frequency as the divine tuning fork; and the more you feel "it", the longer the gaps between the jumps of the needle become. You do this by *Opening Your Heart*. As this is our spiritual default state, unlike our many default states when we operate in the world, it is achieved by *Doing Nothing*. It is more than being passive; it involves the holy (in my opinion) act of Surrender, of opening up to receive. In the spiritual world, I recommend that we be like a beggar. We cannot be anything else because the riches of the spirit are infinitely more fulfilling than the so-called riches of the world, that it is an honour and a privilege to recognize that we have the opportunity to "Ask and it shall be given."

The greatest fool is the one who, when invited to the feast, looks on in awe at the banquet and goes hungry and thirsty while his generous host smiles benevolently in his direction. This lack of uptake disappoints the host; even though he has been called the King of Kings — and because he is — it is his pleasure to bestow grace and favour. Unbeknown to the fool, the ruler of this kingdom delights in opportunities for joyful interaction with his people, his children, and loves to receive their sincere feelings of gratitude and love that arise when they experience and receive far more than they expected. He can only give when asked, so don't forget to ask whenever you sit down to "do nothing", to experience your heart and the love of the creator. *Don't ask for anything in particular, just ask to receive.*

> *"The wisest man in the kingdom of God is the beggar*
> *for he receives untold riches of internal experiences.*
> *Be not too humble to ask!"* (CL)

Scientists tell us that "Nature abhors a vacuum." Well, as paradoxical as it sounds, given that the object and focus of your meditation is vibrating inside every atom of your body, you have to create a vacuum, a space inside yourself, so that you can shift your awareness (and consequently your consciousness) from the finite mental and physical/material dimension to the inner and infinite dimension of the divine, the so-called Kingdom of Heaven. Forgive the clichés, but you create this *space for Grace* by the power of your desire, your *urge to merge*; in other words, by your sincere intent to be open to receive, *without attachment* to what may be experienced. As I will explain in the next chapter, it is not the sensory aspects of your meditation on Spirit or the godhead within that should be your goal, even though they can be mind-blowing and also reassuring for novice meditators, as it was for me, because they confirm the existence of this other reality; however "big" or "small" those aspects are, they act only as a reference point to something far more subtle and far more precious. They are the coat hooks on which you hang your attention in order to allow yourself to be absorbed by divine love, the love the creator has for his most precious creation, you!

CHAPTER THREE

# Going Within: The Aspects and Attributes of Spirit and the Divine

*"The most beautiful thing that we can experience is the mysterious."* (Albert Einstein)

*"Knowing others is wisdom, knowing yourself is Enlightenment."* (Lao Tzu)

*"Close your eyes, fall in Love, stay there!"* (Rumi)

CONSIDER THIS: *You already are "whole", "complete", "one with the divine". It's thinking that stops you from experiencing it — not thinking that you aren't, or even thinking that you are, just thinking, any thinking!*

We have to locate that place that is beyond the mind, so that we can reside there forever, or at least for as long as we can! Remember, Home is where the Heart is! The mind is the originator of virtually all our thoughts, "good" and "bad". Fortunately for us, the good thing about humans is that, even though we are attempting to understand these words by using the mind, our true essence is beyond the mind, and that's why these words of truth will resonate in the heart space of most people.

Yes, our true essence is the divine, the spark of life, the energy inside everything that is created. That vital spark sustains it all, and it can be experienced. Indeed one could say it is each human being's destiny to reconnect and merge with it. Why? Because nothing else is remotely good enough, sufficient or fulfilling.

*"Travel the world and the seven seas, everybody's looking for something."* — Annie Lennox, Eurythmics ("Sweet Dreams (Are Made Of This)")

In this world, the closest we get to experiencing Peace, or Harmony, or relative stillness and a quiet mind, is:

when we are in nature, which has no mind, but reflects the beauty of the created — whether it be majestic scenery, magnificent views, colourful skies or twinkling stars, or the simple perfection of a flower or the gracefulness of a butterfly;

witnessing the miracles of birth or death;

in life-or-death situations where the accompanying fear, risk or peril means we dare not focus our attention and concentration on any other moment but the present;

in other "altered states", e.g. through the rhythm of dance and/or emotion of music and song, or the intensity of sexual union;

and when an unexpected realization or experience takes us through hard set boundaries of the previously familiar, whether they be beliefs, concepts, ideals, rules and codes, or religions.

The meditation I practise always does it for me. I hope that by now you can agree with me that so-called "peace of mind" should more accurately be called "peace *from* mind".

*"It's not Peace **of** Mind we need, it's Peace **from** Mind! Peace lies beyond thought and emotion in a place so still and pure and infinite inside!"* (CL)

*"Enlightenment is the journey from head back to the heart, from words back to silence; getting back to our innocence in spite of our intelligence."* (Ravishankar, spiritual leader)

*"Irony or what?! As long as Mind convinces you to
self-improve it, it keeps you from discovering
the real divine you just beyond its reach!"* (CL)

For those new to the practice of meditation, I suggest
you choose a quiet location indoors and one where you
are unlikely to be disturbed, perhaps your bedroom. I
like to have the room as dark as possible, so you may
wish to close curtains or blinds. By all means light a
candle or tea-light — you certainly won't be meditating
on its flame as your whole purpose is to go within
inside of yourself, and the less outside distractions, the
better; if you prefer a lit candle to complete darkness in
your room, then light it also as a mark of respect to the
Giver, and as a symbol of your opening up to receive
(no flame without the presence of oxygen), rather than
as a representation of the divine light with which you
seek to merge.

Sit on the floor or on the bed with your back straight.
To help achieve this, it is a good idea to position your
backside only, i.e. not your legs, on one or two cushions
or pillows; it is also recommended that you sit away
from the wall, headboard or bedstead so that you avoid
leaning or supporting your back, otherwise you will
enter a different altered state, that of sleep, if you are
tired. As physically nourishing as this may be, it defeats
the spiritual purpose of your meditation. As with most
skills and practices, start by creating good habits and
avoid the bad ones. It is better to sit cross-legged than

with your legs stretched out as you need to maintain a straight back. For those who can sit in the lotus position comfortably, that would be ideal. Regarding what to do with your hands, you could let them flop down into your lap, but I recommend resting them on your knees. You could have them open, as in "open to receive", but I prefer joining the tips of the thumb and forefinger together to form a circle, with the remaining fingers relaxed — that's what works for me! Because you then need to have your eyes closed, please read the next few paragraphs so that you know what to do and what to expect. Repeat for each "aspect".

With your eyes closed, take a few long calming breaths with the dual intent of letting go of the junk that has already accumulated in your mind that day, as well as purifying and preparing your body to feel. It would help at this time to remember your experiences with *A Glimpse* to remind you of your non-earthbound potential, and I recommend you listen to this session in the twenty-four hours before you practise meditation for the first two or three times.

After allowing your breathing to then slow down for a couple of minutes, become aware that you are being breathed, and remain as passive and as still as you can.

*"Did you know that each breath is a gift, that you were being breathed and are being breathed? (And will be breathed, God willing!) Most people go through their whole life completely unaware of this God-given miracle."* (CL)

*"I have died many times, but your breath made
me alive again."* (Rumi)

Once you are aware of the breath coming into and
out of your body and breathing you, then that is a good
time to Ask to Receive (see Chapter Two). At this point
there may be felt an accompanying peace and/or stillness
to your act of surrender. Continue to feel your heart
asking to receive by focusing your attention on the big
circle around your heart chakra in the centre of your
chest. With practice, you will experience this whole area
vibrating with wonderful energy as you start to go inside
and leave physical body awareness behind.

By this time, if not before, or indeed throughout,
because you are getting into experiencing something
new (yet older than you), the mind will be racing like
anything! One of my favourite humorous sayings is: *"If
you think the art of conversation is dead, just try telling a child
it's time for bed."* I read that, laughed, then noticed how true
it was when hours later I told my two young children it
was their bedtime! I then realized how they must have
been playing me for a long time as they came up with
interesting questions for me to answer. You too will begin
to relate to this experience as soon as you tell your own
mischievous child of a mind that it's time to disappear.

Keep your mind at a distance if you can. Initially this
may be difficult to do as it will comment on anything

and everything, from "Am I doing this right? / You're not doing this right!" to "Wow, that was amazing!!" My advice is to imagine each and every moment as a train platform. Stay on the platform! As thoughts manifest, let them pass through, no matter how relevant, informative or entertaining they may be. Do not get on the train! Not only will this train of thoughts take you away from your destination that lies inside the stillness of the present moment, but you will run out of track and find yourself lost in wasteland, successfully derailed by your mind from your objective of going beyond it. Remember, to go beyond the mind you need to slow down and be still enough to connect with the other dimension that lies beyond time and matter, and that is achieved by withdrawing attention from the outer world and opening up to the absolute reality within.

That reality, the inner world of Spirit, has at least four tangible, almost physical, attributes. These are visual, auditory, kinaesthetic and gustatory (seeing, hearing, feeling, taste), and sometimes olfactory (smell). I am now going to talk about each one in turn with regard to their individual attributes and other associated benefits as experienced by me over a period spanning five decades. I hope that in doing so, you will be able to appreciate the vastness and essence of the life energy inside of you and go on to experience the joy that comes from fulfilling Life's true purpose.

## Visual (Sight) / Light, aka "Divine Light"

*"God is Light, and in Him there is no darkness at all."*
(John 1:5)

*"Close both eyes to see with the other eye."* (Rumi)

*"If thine eye be single thy whole body shall be full of Light."*
(Matthew 6:22)

*"He who throws heart's doors wide open
can see the sun in every atom."* (Rumi)

*"Although you appear in earthly form,
your essence is pure Consciousness.
You are the fearless guardian of Divine Light."* (Rumi)

*"There is a Secret One inside us; the planets in all the
galaxies pass through his hands like beads. That is a string
of beads one should look at with luminous eyes."* (Kabir)

*"The universe and the light of the stars come through me."*
(Rumi)

I cannot stress enough to you that this divine light
written about in many scriptures, especially in reference
to God, is NOT symbolic. When the many Masters, Jesus
included, "revealed" themselves to their sincere followers,
they did so by connecting them to the divinity inside each

soul. Can you imagine just what a powerful experience it must be to be shown a light shining brightly inside your head? Seeing this divine light inside you would surely go a long way to accepting that the giver of such a miracle could actually be God's representative on Earth. As Jesus himself said: *"Beware of false prophets, which come to you in sheep's clothing, but inwardly they are ravening wolves. Ye shall know them by their fruits."* (Matthew 7:15 & 16).

Experiencing the Light of God in meditation, inside you and therefore inside the whole of creation as well as inside the vast empty space that is inside every atom, is literally mind-blowing. Much more fulfilling however is the Love that is felt as you look at the Light. This cannot be said by me enough times — *all these aspects of God are just portals to the Love that emanates for you and through you as you open up to receive.*

There are times when I "see" hardly any Light at all, just a pleasing glow; at other times, it is blinding. Irrespective of the brightness of that Light, the gift that is constant is the connection of Love. It's an infinite ocean into which you can dive as deep as your thirst will allow.

So, once you are settled in your body and the volume of your mind is barely noticeable, then start your meditation with the Light. Ask to receive, and with your eyes remaining closed, imagine peering into the Universe inside your head, reminding yourself that *each sub-atomic particle contains the same universe that it is an infinitesimally small part of.* And that everything in its essence is Light. Is, not was or will be, but is; and that

185

Light is felt as the purest Love. If you want to follow the advice given by Jesus to "let thine eye be single" in order to focus your attention, then imagine that the inside edges of the corneas of your two physical eyes form the corners of the base line of a triangle, and that the top corner is in the centre of your forehead. You can then focus attention on this so-called third eye, imagining it is facing within and seeing the subtle emanation of divine Light. Soon the Light can appear more brightly, sometimes as a "divine donut" or ring shape where the dark inside can suddenly become far brighter than the outside, and you are immediately travelling through it into a universe of Light, and Light is all you can see; at other times the experience is not as dramatic, and yet the experience of the interconnectedness of all things and the feeling of love behind it all that empowers it, and specifically the creator's love for you inside your soul, is the most beautiful emotion you can have and doesn't seem to depend on how much Light you are seeing. Just the simple act of putting yourself in that state of grace by asking to receive (which I guess is the whole point of meditation) allows the love to fill your heart. Because there is no other human emotion like it, I have to call it Divine Emotion or Divine Love. This experience is not only accessible via meditation, as I shall explain later.

> *"A light came and kindled a flame in the depth of my soul.*
> *A light so radiant that the sun orbits around it*
> *like a butterfly."* (Rumi)

*"The Supreme soul is seen within the soul.*
*The Point is seen within the Supreme soul.*
*And within the Point, the reflection is seen again.*
*Kabir is blest because he has this supreme vision!"* (Kabir)

*"The eye with which I see God is the same with which*
*God sees me. My eye and God's eye is one eye, one sight, one*
*knowledge, one love."*
(Meister Eckhart, 14th Century German mystic)

*"The light which shines in the eye*
*Is really the light of the heart.*
*The light which fills the heart is the light of God,*
*which is pure*
*And separate from the light of intellect and sense."* (Rumi)

At first you may only be able to hold this awareness for five minutes; with regular practice see if you can build it up to ten or fifteen minutes.

There have been times when the Light can be seen outside of formal meditation. For example, there are times that I have walked into a dark room and the Light is reassuringly there. It doesn't light the room as a flashlight would, but its presence is welcoming. There are many times when I'm having a shower that the Light is there — well they do say that "Cleanliness is next to Godliness"!

There have also been times in formal meditation when the Light has been exceptionally pure and bright, for example when I was staying in the house of a humble fellow meditator, her home was one of the holiest places I have ever had the good fortune to visit. Another time, I was sat meditating in my bedroom at my parents' house just before my younger twin brother's and sister's big birthday party. The vibration of love was very strong, and when I'd "finished" meditating on the Light, I opened my eyes to see a figure of light in the room. I couldn't see a face, but the figure of light remained "standing" at the foot of the bed for a long time. It was then that I realized that I was still seeing the Light, and that maybe this is how angels appeared to humans. After the party, my brother and sister criticized me because many of their friends had complained to them that "it was as if Costa was on drugs", despite the fact that they knew I was vegetarian and didn't drink or smoke, let alone take drugs. The after-effects of my meditation had lasted all night. I will talk more about these "BOOMS times" in the next chapter.

*"Shall I play with words when love has the space inside me filled with light?"* (Kabir)

It is almost common knowledge these days that we all come from the Light, and that the Light is where we return and where we "belong". Witness exorcisms, or even Spirit Releasement sessions, where ghosts, malevolent spirits or inhabiting entities are entreated to "go into the Light." Also, those of us who have had NDEs (Near Death Experiences) will talk about being drawn into the Light and the wonderfully loving feelings associated with "the other side". Light is Love. I remember listening to one NDEer's account on *Oprah* which I found so inspiring because I could relate to it completely. This gentleman had experienced a heart attack whilst at his desk in the hospital where he worked. Although he had "died", he explained how the medics "went the extra mile" because they knew him, and had tried to revive him at his desk rather than risk losing him for sure on the way to the emergency room. They succeeded, but while "dead" he experienced the beauty of the bright Light, and the immense peace, serenity, love and sense of homecoming that accompany it. So powerful and life-altering was his experience that, as he explained, "I now get far more satisfaction from opening the door for someone than I used to get from closing a business deal."

We are all blessed to have opportunities whilst still alive to merge with the Light that shines brightly inside our heads, to feel the love that emanates from the Source, and to recognize the divinity inside all others.

*"You have no need to travel anywhere, journey within yourself. Enter a mine of rubies and bathe in the splendour of your own light."* (Rumi)

*"If all that glittered were gold,
it still would not be as bright or as precious as
the Light in your soul. Let Heart guide you home!"* (CL)

*"Nothing can nourish the soul but light."* (Rumi)

*"I wish I could show you, when you are lonely or in darkness, the astonishing light of your own being."* (Hafiz, 14th Century Persian mystic poet)

*"Let your heart's light guide you to my home. Let your heart's light show you that we are one."* (Rumi)

*"Become the Light."* (Rumi)

## Auditory (Hearing) / Sound, aka Music, Harmony, or "the Music of the Spheres"

*"If you want the truth, I'll tell you the truth: Listen to the secret sound, the real sound, which is inside you."* (Kabir)

*"When I am silent, I fall into the place where everything is music."* (Rumi)

This is the second aspect of the divine. It is important to practise each aspect individually and not at the same time as any of the others, if possible. When you have sat down to meditate, and after seeing and feeling the Light, if mind and body are still enough, and there are no noisy distractions, you will find it easier to concentrate on the sound within the silence! Depending on your environment, it may greatly assist your requirement to concentrate and focus inside if you wear large headphones that cover your ears or small headphones or earplugs lightly inserted in the ears. If these headphones are connected to any equipment, ensure it is turned off or disconnect them. Keep your body still, and become aware (or remind yourself) that every particle of energy and matter, no matter how microscopically small, contains not only Light but also Sound. Listen out for that sound, the so-called Music of the Spheres. It is the auditory manifestation of the vibration of Life and Love inside the whole of creation. In listening to it, it has the power to slow down the most active of minds, but first there has to be the leap from Doing to Being, from disidentifying with your outer form and seeking to merge with your inner form and the Oneness — be the grateful beggar, and once again ask to receive.

When you first start to hear these tones or harmonics, you will be convinced that they must be coming from your outside environment, and there is a tendency to want to shift your attention and concentration from inside to outside rather than remaining in the moment being absorbed by the beauty of the Music. In my first few weeks of meditation, I used to attribute the higher-pitched tones to the slow squeaking movement of railway stock from the tracks about three miles away from my lodgings that I'd been used to hearing before, and I would turn my attention from inside listening to outside listening in order to confirm this. In nearly all cases I was mistaken, and I began to accept the wonders of the divine experience within inside of me. As with "seeing" the Light, you may find when listening to the Music that it is accompanied by an overwhelming sense of the creator's love for you that inspires reverence and love in you for "him".

*"The flute of the infinite is played without ceasing
and its sound is love."* (Kabir)

*"I am the hole on the flute that God's breath flows through.
Listen to this music."* (Hafiz)

Meditating on the inner music is the antidote to a racing mind. If you have been "in your head" for most of the day, it has the capability of stilling your mind and soothing your soul.

*"As long as I talked unceasingly about the Lord,
The Lord stayed away, kept at a distance.
But when I silenced my mouth, and sat very still
And fixed my mind at the doorway of the Lord,
I was linked to the music of the Word,
And all my talking came to an end."* (Kabir)

*"Angelic music is endlessly pouring down from heaven, are
you in a state to hear it?"* (Rumi)

*"Music without words means leaving behind the mind.
And leaving behind the mind is meditation.
Meditation returns you to the source.
And the source of all is sound."* (Kabir)

## Kinaesthetic (Feeling) / Primordial Vibration, aka Holy Name or "The Word"

This third aspect of the divine has always been, for me, the most powerful, the deepest and strongest connector to God. It is the felt presence of the Holy Spirit inside of you, and what makes it most remarkable is that, unlike Light and Music, it can be experienced any time, i.e. outside of formal meditation. Taking specific time out for meditation though is essential in maintaining a strong connection throughout the rest of the day with the Holy Name.

At the risk of offending some followers of Christianity and Hinduism, I can tell you that "The Word of God" is not the Bible, and it is not "Om" either!

*"In the beginning was the Word, and the Word was with God, and the Word was God. The same was in the beginning with God. All things were made by him, and without him was not any thing made that was made."*
(John 1: 1-3)

John is telling us that there is a Primordial Vibration that allows everything to be — it is inside the building blocks of the Universe. It has no form in the same way that Love has no form, and it has no boundary. Scientists may be able to show you cells, molecules and atoms moving and vibrating at their core, but their minds can only take them to the boundaries of mass/matter and to the now scientifically acceptable concept of "Energy". Inside your body, and beyond your mind, you have a heart. Minds can only guess, speculate, theorize and believe, whereas *Hearts feel and **know**!* Love is not a concept. *It is Love that sustains Energy — your atoms may be vibrating with it but your cells can't feel it; your mind has no means of knowing it; only your Heart completely gets it.* Until your heart experiences it (again), you are a lost soul looking for it in relationships, materialism and everything else that the world has to offer.

> *"It is love that holds everything together.*
> *And it's the everything too."* (Rumi)

> *"Love hertz! When you are vibrating at the frequency*
> *of Love then you are fulfilling your life's purpose.*
> *Tune in with your Heart."* (CL)

> *"Love said to me 'There is nothing that is not me.*
> *Be silent.'"* (Rumi)

> *"Every thing has a name, and its Name is Love."* (CL)

To experience the true Name of God and the Holy Spirit, first of all you need to ensure that you are following the advice I gave earlier about body posture. Now that you have been listening to Music, your mind should be very still and therefore you should find it easier to focus on your breathing, i.e. that you are being breathed. As you go deeply into the breath, and where this breath is coming from, time soon becomes still and you find yourself at the point of perfection — no longer body or mind, but a vessel for the divine. You have entered the House of God inside your own body and are merging with Spirit. How do you know this? Although you may be aware of vibrations around your chest and heart chakra, this is the only "physical" awareness of a body that you have, you are now Love and nothing else exists! That creator's love, sustaining the universe and behind each breath, is felt in your heart and you cannot feel anything else — you are now Home, literally in Heaven! When the mystical poets attempted to express their experiences of "the greatest love", and of truth, consciousness and bliss; when the prophets and spiritual teachers told us *That which you are looking for is within inside of you*"; when Jesus said *"The kingdom of God is within you"* (Luke 17:21), this is what they were talking about!

*"The Father spoke one Word, which was his Son, and this Word he speaks always in eternal silence, and in silence must it be heard by the Soul."* (Verse 100, Sayings of Light and Love by Saint John of the Cross, 16th century Spanish mystic)

*"Because your sighs have fermented my blood, I need no wine."* (Rumi)

*"The one no-one talks of speaks the secret sound to himself,
and he's the one who's made it all."* (Kabir)

*"In your light I learn how to love.
In your beauty, how to make poems.
You dance inside my chest,
Where no-one sees you."* (Rumi)

*"Breath. So, so underrated! Behind each one is what your
heart and soul want you to pay attention to, your divine
eternal life force. Be still my love!"* (CL)

*"That which God said to the rose,
And caused it to laugh in full-blown beauty,
He said to my heart,
And made it a hundred times more beautiful."* (Rumi)

*"You will find me in the tiniest house of time.
Kabir says: Student, tell me, what is God?
He is the breath inside the breath."* (Kabir)

*"I smile like a flower not only with my lips
But with my whole being
For I am alone with the King
And have lost myself in him."* (Rumi)

*"WHERE does this moment come from??
By all means think about it. Better still to FEEL it…"
#Love #Grace #Consciousness* (CL)

*"Now that you live here in my chest,
anywhere we sit is a mountain top."* (Rumi)

At first this divine experience may only last a few seconds or minutes before the mind regains your attention and drags you back to your other identity in the material world, but with practice you will be able to spend more time in God consciousness and less time in your head. As you do so, you begin to recognize that *this connection directly affects the quality of your life*. More about this in the next chapter.

## Gustatory (Taste) / Nectar

*"In the inner wine cellar I drank of my Beloved, and when
I went abroad through all this valley I no longer knew
anything, and lost the herd that I was following."* (Verse 26,
Sayings of Light and Love, John of the Cross)

*"I drank that wine of which the soul is its vessel.
Its ecstasy has stolen my intellect away."* (Rumi)

Yes, as unbelievable as it sounds, you can "taste God", or at least experience that there is yet another sensory aspect to the divine essence, the Spirit inside your physical body. Inside your head there is a flow of sweet-tasting nectar. It is well-hidden because we are only taught about the presence of saliva in the mouth and mucus in the nose and throat, but it is there nevertheless. Just the action and intent of looking for it with my tongue is sufficient to centre me deeply, by which I mean, to put me into God-consciousness and awareness of my true form. Over and above this altered state, getting to also occasionally experience the taste of Nectar is for me a bonus, the "cherry on the cake".

When you connect with it, you feel centred and strong. As well as these attributes (great for enabling you to remove tight-fitting lids off jars!), it has the added benefit for me of also connecting me with the third aspect of the divine, the Holy Name. I especially love to centre myself and experience the gustatory and kinaesthetic aspects of the divine whenever I am driving, or in any other solitary activity where talking or eating is not required, if and when I remember to. I also find it a natural way of continuing to experience the bliss after getting up from a formal meditation.

There have been many times when I have been practising this technique walking through a crowd of shoppers in a busy mall, feeling completely connected with my heart and the creator's love, and at deep peace within myself; I have felt like an invisible alien (or rather a human being), barely noticeable to others (the human doings), yet so full of love for my fellow Earth dwellers.

Although it may have taken me many months to succeed more consistently in tasting Nectar when looking for it, I have also experienced the extremely rare occurrence of being able to smell the most beautiful fragrance inside my mouth and nostrils. For me this has only occurred four or five times, and it has usually happened while tasting Nectar. Each time it was such an overpowering sensation that I had to look to see if there were any flowers in my location. One time, there were flowers, but the gorgeous aroma stayed with me when I walked out of that room and far away; another time I experienced it in my car, not the world's likeliest location for attractive odours! A fellow meditator friend of mine who had also experienced it described it as the scent of the gardenia flower, but I wouldn't know; all I know is that it was intoxicating to me and that I couldn't imagine a more gorgeous fragrance.

> *"My body is flooded with the flame of Love.*
> *My soul lives in a furnace of bliss.*
> *Love's fragrance fills my mouth,*
> *And fans through all things with each breath out."* (Kabir)

And here below, Saint Kabir speaks of the other aspects of the divine in his "Light of the Sun". He alludes to the divine Light in the first line, the Word in the second, Music and Light in the third, and Nectar in the fourth:

> *"There, millions of lamps of sun and moon are burning;*
> *There the drum beats, and the lover swings in play.*
> *There, love songs resound, and light runs in showers;*
> *And the worshipper is entranced in the taste of*
> *heavenly nectar."* (Kabir)

To recap, there are five tangible aspects to experiencing the divine. What makes the experience unmistakably God is the love that flows, gushes and transports you into the realms of true bliss. As I mentioned before, these tangible and real internally experienced sensory components of the Oneness are the coat hooks on which you place your subtle awareness in order for the current of love that permeates all to become a tidal wave of felt love. "Practice makes perfect", so keep practising and merge with the perfection!

*"I looked in temples, churches and mosques.*
*But I found the Divine within my heart."* (Rumi)

*"Value this human body beyond the world's perceptions*
*of 'ugly', 'attractive', or 'sexy'. It is the receptacle*
*for the divine, the meeting place of the finite with*
*the infinite, and without it your soul would have no*
*opportunity to fulfil your life's purpose."* (CL)

*"Remember, the entrance door to the sanctuary*
*is inside you."* (Rumi)

*"Enter God's kingdom via your Heart.*
*Once there, you discover there is no place and no thing,*
*just an infinite ocean of Love."* (CL)

*"Between the Mountains of Moments*
*Lies the Valley of Deep Peace.*

Let Heart's Breath glide you Home
To float on the Eternal Path of Bliss." (CL)

"Have you found the OFF switch to your Mind?
There isn't one! You have to disappear where it can't follow
into the Love and Light of your soul." (CL)

"In the inner stillness where meditation leads, the Spirit
secretly anoints the soul and heals our deepest wounds."
(Saint John of the Cross)

"Even Nature, in all her glory, cannot compare with the
beauty inside of you." (CL)

"The very centre of your heart is where life begins.
The most beautiful place on Earth." (Rumi)

"The sacred place you are looking for is within you.
Let all your actions come from here so that you may
better serve humanity." (CL)

"What is the body? That shadow of a shadow of your love,
that somehow contains the entire universe." (Rumi)

"In the deep inner stillness of the Heart is found
the haven of perfect peace and unconditional love.
With humility and reverence, step inside and
kiss your divine self!" (CL)

*"Attention please! The journey of Life involves turning
all senses within to connect and Be, not Do.
Attention In, not Out!"* (CL)

*"Your secret admirer, your one true lover, is waiting for you
inside. Shut the doors to the outside world and meet in the
heart."* (CL)

*"All know that the drop merges into the ocean, but few know
that the ocean merges into the drop."* (Kabir)

*"The Doorway. Each moment provides a doorway
into the Heart. Will you step off the well trodden path of
thoughts to meet with your Beloved?"* (CL)

*"Sacred Solitude. Take time out every day to sit in Spirit,
bathe in your Light and feel the divine Love vibrate
in your Heart. Come Home!"* (CL)

*"I am lost in God, and God is found in me.
Why look in all directions? Look inside."* (Rumi)

*"The 'problem' with Enlightenment is not attaining it
but maintaining it! Hence the expression
'Practice makes Perfect.'"* (CL)

In the following chapter I speak from personal experience about some of the benefits and challenges of leading an "inner life".

But now, as the promised Post Script to the Self-Esteem session in Chapter Ten of Part One, I will describe an alternative means of maintaining strength, focus, presence, confidence and control in very demanding situations. It comes courtesy of my good friend and fellow Manchester-based healer Coby Zvikler, the inventor of the Empower Disc and of the Pain Control Chip for mobile phones.

If you recall, we talked not only about the interconnectedness of all things, but also about the holographic principle: that everything that is outside is also inside. Indeed, I had experienced the universe inside of me when practising meditating on the Divine Light.

Whenever you find yourself in a situation that makes you nervous, e.g. a formal presentation or a conflict-type scenario, then just imagine that the whole of that room / location is inside you, is inside your body (with your "little body" and its surroundings inside your "bigger body"). In this way, you become almost an observer of what is happening. Because of this detachment from the emotional symptoms, or because you have now become more spiritually aware, you are allowing the scene to be played out, providing you with an inner strength, almost a "knowing" of how to react and perform in each and every moment as the scene unfolds. Try it out the next time a situation is sprung on you!

# CHAPTER FOUR

# Life as a Conscious Being

*"Each breath is not taken, it is given. It is given with Love. The Question is: 'Is it received with love?'"* (Costa Lambrias)

*"Heaven and Hell. Hell is just a state of Mind, Heaven a state of Heart. Which state do you currently live in?"* (Costa Lambrias)

*"Love comes calling with every breath. Are you In or Out?"* (Costa Lambrias)

*"The world is no more than the Beloved's single face; in
the desire of the One to know its own beauty, we exist."*
(Ghalib, 19th Century Urdu and Persian poet)

W E ARE BILLIONS OF SOULS, all fragments of the One
Soul which is Spirit/God consciousness expressing
itself.

Just think about that statement and what it means.
Each one of us on this particular planet is an essential part
of the Creator's divine game to know itself. Given that
everything created was done so out of Love, then Love is
our destiny, by which I mean we are all pre-programmed
for Truth, Consciousness, and Bliss. Just as there is a
program inside each salmon that drives it to return
upstream to its source, its birthplace; and a "knowing"
inside birds that drives them to cross continents to
migrate, so we humans are similarly programmed for
Love, to seek to merge with our self, or rather, to discover
our true self. Along life's journey, we usually look for
that love in others first before looking for it within inside
of ourselves.

In life, we learn to compromise. I am not suggesting
this is "wrong" or "bad"; what I am saying is that our
divine essence, the God inside Life that creates and
sustains all, will not be satisfied until it returns to Source,
until it knows itself. The raising of our Consciousness is
a vital component in taking us closer to that "goal" and
in maintaining our experience of it. Right now, on this
planet and for the sake of humanity, it is not enough for

me and you to be aware of who and what we are, and why we all are here; not only do we have to bathe in our divine light, listen to our harmonic resonance, and vibrate at the frequency of the Holy Name, but the best service we can do for our fellow travellers is to remind them also of their divine purpose.

*"Strive not to be a success, but rather to be of value."*
(Albert Einstein)

Unconsciousness is responsible for all the ills we are experiencing on this planet. We may call or refer to it as: greed, lust for power, selfishness, poverty, strife, patriotism / war, insecurity, or ego; but all these and others are symptoms of the cause: a lack of spiritual awareness that manifests as seeing others as separate from me.

Once you bathe in your true divine form and recognize the essence that sustains all, including people with whom you previously had nothing in common, then, theoretically, you should mellow and feel a higher love for others that transcends all boundaries and differences. I say "theoretically" because very often I still find it difficult to not get in my head and react to displays of lack of consideration for others exhibited by politicians, abusers, and occasionally even road users. Somewhat ironically, any displays of lack of awareness when driving by other road users, or lack of consideration to others in the way they manoeuvre, turn, or position their vehicles without indicating their intent, has sometimes initially resulted in a loss of awareness on my part of that driver's divine essence. That is life, and also my challenge, one which I am steadily winning.

It's easy to be at peace and in divine consciousness when meditating or doing nothing. The challenge for me, and I guess for all of us, is to maintain the divine connection and remain rooted in solid peace, when others and circumstances push our buttons.

Albert Camus, the French existential writer, refers to something like this in "The Plague" (*La Peste*). Ironically, his reference occurs in the only part of the book that at each time of reading as a student made no sense to me (I read it at least five times as it was my favourite book when I studied French literature).

The two main protagonists, Tarrou and Rieux, are discussing their fight against the plague that is killing the townsfolk of Oran which has now been cut off from the rest of the world. (Analogies here of the fight of the Resistance against the Nazis, Good versus Evil, pre-dating Star Wars' Jedi versus Sith, Light versus Dark.) Tarrou, whose means of earning a living were never made clear but were possibly morally dubious, says: "I want to know how to become a saint." The kindly Doctor Rieux responds: "What interests me is to be a man." "Yes, we are searching for the same thing," says Tarrou, "but I am less ambitious."

For many years I had lived an ascetic lifestyle as a renunciate. Life in the ashram (shelter from the world) was purposefully simple: Satsang (words of Truth), Service, and Meditation. Merging with God was a daily reality. In this lifestyle, there were no emotions apart from the divine experiences of love and bliss. Looking back, I had been living in an ivory tower, far removed from the day-to-day experiences of the rest of society. When the ashrams closed and I had to negotiate how to survive in the world without that shelter, I also rediscovered boy-girl relationships and therefore emotions! I was nevertheless shocked to discover that people got depressed, even those who lived in idyllic locations such as my parents' birthplace, the paradise island of Cyprus. Life had certainly been easier as a "saint". The challenge now was for me to integrate back into society and to make a positive contribution as a "normal" human being. Tarrou's remark began to make sense.

There have been two constants throughout my spiritual life. One has been the presence of a teacher (more about this in the next chapter), the other has been the experience of fulfilment that comes from reconnecting to Source by turning my attention inwards. All it takes is for me to remember to do so! In death we are that divine form, our challenge is a daily one: to remember to take time out from where our mind wants to take us, and to merge with God consciousness whilst still in physical form.

*"While your heart sings the song of the divine*
*The senses seek to distract you without.*
*Be still for a moment,*
*And ride the waves of Love!"* (CL)

*"Home is where the Heart is. Heart is where your true
Home is. Heart misses you, come home!"* (CL)

*"Mesmerized. Hypnotized. Enraptured. Blissing Out.
Love comes calling with every breath.
Are you In or Out?"* (CL)

There have been many times when I have sat down
to do nothing else but merge and the results have been
the most beautiful meditations, ones filled with love and
bliss. I call these my "BOOMS" times, as in "Blissed Out
Of My Skull"! These BOOMS times invariably result in
a continuation in the experience of bliss, and of the love
that creates, sustains and maintains all matter, atoms
and molecules and their interconnectedness to each
other, especially to all other life forms. I remember one
particularly powerful meditation, after which I caught
a bus and tube train to take me to work. As I walked
into work, some of my co-workers noticed that I didn't
appear to be my usual happy, cheerful and smiling self.
"Are you alright Costa?" my concerned friends enquired.
"I'm fine, really I am," I mumbled, such was the effort I
begrudgingly made in order to answer them. I couldn't
really tell them that every single physical step I had
taken since getting up from meditation had been, and
continued to be, accompanied by an atom bomb of the
most intense bliss exploding everywhere inside. My
serious demeanour concealed a universe of love inside
of me that I was still connected to and grateful for. I am

blessed with these BOOMS times only a few times a year. Far rarer have been the occasions when they have continued throughout the whole night when sleep normally would have overtaken me. I have felt such a connection to the divine in a wonderful and seemingly endless exchange of receiving and giving love, that my body has felt more like a vibration than a physical form. Needless to say, this was far more replenishing to body and soul than the rest that normal sleep provides.

*"Although I may try to describe Love, when I experience it, I am speechless."* (Rumi)

In "the good old days" of the ashram, it would not be unusual for me to sit down during a short lunch break at work to meditate as deeply as I could on the Holy Name. On one occasion when I had sat outside in the yard, I felt my back straightening and lengthening, my head rising, and a huge surge of energy shooting all the way up my spine and out of my head, accompanied by blissful love for me. I felt incredible, walking tall and buzzing with the same energy for the rest of the day. It was a number of years later that I read about this so-called kundalini energy.

NOTHING IS REAL! Knowing this provides you with a spiritual perspective that acts as a firewall when the dramas of your existence would otherwise affect your inner peace. And if the purpose of our life is to be connected to Source, to be conscious of our true divine nature, then any "setback", "failure" or "disaster" (as the non-conscious world perceives it) is just *a reminder to be conscious*. It's all a blessing; it may even help bring unconscious people closer to asking the more spiritually appropriate questions about the real purpose of their existence, which in turn may bring them closer to the truth.

*"Existence and Life. The difference between just existing and truly living is a matter of Consciousness as one is done "inside out" and the other "outside in". So, where is YOUR attention going?"* (CL)

*"Everything will be an alien experience for you until you experience that the centre of the Universe and Creation is inside your Heart."* (CL)

*"Illusion. The act of mistaking that everything outside of you is real. Enlightenment. Experiencing the divine inside and out!"* (CL)

IT'S ALL INSIDE! The dimension of the true reality can only be accessed inside. Death of the body is one way of accessing it, mind-expanding stimulants another; both are extreme and unnecessary. Consciousness of the love behind each given breath is sufficient (and a preferable alternative?).

The outer world then becomes your playground because the inner universe provides you with your true identity, that of a formless being (soul) whose essence is divine, that of Spirit, Love and Light. Bathing in your true essence via regular meditation provides you with the security and resilience required to see you through challenging times and situations as they occur in the outside world — in your work, home life, and globally.

On long and weary days when I find myself caught up in my worldly identity, it helps for me to look up at the sky, especially at night when the stars are visible. This reminds me that there are more universes, with their own galaxies and sun systems, than there are grains of sand on planet Earth. A very impressive statistic, especially when you consider that there are probably a million grains in a fistful of sand, and many more millions times fistfuls on any one beach, and then God knows how many beaches on this planet. Many years ago, in my late teenage years, this truth would have been enough to trigger the feelings I talked about of despair, isolation and futility of existence, but instead I now feel the love that sustains every molecule of creation vibrating so strongly within my body that I feel genuinely blessed and so much gratitude for this divine connection.

*"I just want to thank the creator for letting me know.
Now that I know how beautiful and full of divine love
everything is, I feel complete."* (CL)

And yet each one of us seemingly insignificant specks, on an equally insignificant speck of a planet, in an insignificant universe, in the vastness of space / creation, acts as if I am the main player and that everything is centred around me. On one level, this is true! That's how important you are, and I sincerely hope you can appreciate the love and care that is behind all of that creation that was brought into being so that you could achieve your birthright, the actual purpose to your existence.

On another level, however, most of us are unaware of our true nature, and therefore experience our existence and life on this planet as Separate from all other beings. I don't mean separate from other species or creatures, I mean separate from each other. This "forgetfulness" of our true essence and the actual potential for universal consciousness means that we exist as separated fragments of the whole, identifying only with our own desires, thoughts and wants — in other words, the universe revolves around me, the ego, and not around you or anyone else.

As I've said before, this complete and utter lack of consciousness, of spiritual awareness, manifests as all the major problems in this world right now, whether they be humanitarian or environmental. If I see you as separate from me, then I am more inclined to attack you if someone from your country, separate state or different culture, may have insulted me or my country or culture; or if you are part of a different religion or ideology than mine. This is madness! And it is happening every day somewhere in this world. And not just between different doctrines and belief systems thousands of miles apart, but even within so-called communities and families; old to young, there are no age restrictions to Ignorance.

When I studied Nutrition, one of the important fundamental requirements of the human body we were taught about was hydration. To hammer this home to any client who wasn't drinking enough water, we would draw a big circle on a sheet of paper to represent one cell. We would then explain that our body is made up of billions of these cells which are themselves 99.9% water. Then we would scrawl tiny zigzag lines all around the outside of the circle. We would explain that these represented cholesterol that had formed in order to maintain the integrity of the cell and to stop it from completely hardening; and with billions and billions of cells, each one feeling isolated, no wonder on a macroscopic level the client might feel isolated, stressed, depressed, or even suicidal.

The above is a perfect analogy to illustrate the madness in this world, the separateness, the identification with "I" and "You". And just as easily as the benefits of water (which for most societies is far cheaper and more accessible than the commercial world's so-called "real thing" that has no nutritionally positive effect on the body) have only recently been advocated, so there is available to you an infinite source of Consciousness right inside of yourself. It is beyond thought, and reconnecting with it is your default state, an experience that is way beyond anything that anyone can offer you from this world. Yes, I am talking about your Spirit, that essence which when it leaves with your soul so does your breath, and thus your life in this world ends.

It has been with you all your life, ignored by you most of the time, waiting patiently for you to return your awareness to it, still loving you with every breath that is given, while you continue to identify with *everything else but it*: your mind, your body, your senses, your goals and your aspirations in this world. And the closest many of us have gotten to it up until now is in those breath-taking moments of beauty provided by Nature where everything is still and quiet and the mind may find it difficult to continue its chatter, and what is outside of you strikes a chord with what is inside of you; or in extreme sports or activities which require one moment after another of utter focus, and where a lapse in concentration might mean injury or death; or at the time of death; or when words of truth are being expressed and recognition of those truths is being "felt" once again.

The experience of your true self lies beyond thought and is a timeless one, and is only one breath away!

Did you miss it?

Again? (Sorry, I can't resist reminding you!)

This is the experience that will save mankind and this planet from its rollercoaster journey of self-destruction. Peace isn't the absence of War, it's a *felt* experience, one that each and every human being seeks, but has been looking for outside and not within. Once you are reconnected to the source, the consciousness within, you naturally experience that the same consciousness is operating in every other living entity, and that *we are all the same,* carriers of that same precious Spirit, the energy and awareness inside all matter that sustain it with love. What I mean by "with love" is that when you reconnect with it, you discover that it is giving without wanting anything in return, just happy for you that you are experiencing your true state of being; also, bathing in that infinite pool of the creator's love for you is sometimes experienced as vibrating with bliss — it goes far beyond the world's offerings of "happiness" and "joy".

> *"The source of Life in you, the world and the universe is what makes all of us One. Consciousness of this power leads to the purest Love and Bliss."* (CL)

It's man's acceptance of *everything but* the existence of this infinite Oneness that perpetuates Difference and Separation in the world, socially, politically, culturally, and so on. How ironic it is that wars have been fought and millions killed in the name of God rather than in the name of Greed or Insecurity — Religion does have a lot to answer for. I believe that Religion has probably succeeded in diverting many thousands times more people from an actual direct experience of God than the relatively few of us — whether brought up with or without faith — who have an internal direct connection that they can access whenever they remember to. These fortunate ones have no need of faith or belief because they can be said to Know. Knowing the incontrovertible truth, because you have experienced it, goes beyond Belief. Most people invest in Belief because they want to go to Heaven and not the other place. If you have experienced it, and therefore you know, then Belief becomes a symptom or side-effect of Knowing and doesn't rely on Faith, which is what most Believers without an experience have to depend on.

Reconnecting with Source, either through formal meditation or from remembering to do so, brings a childlike wonder to each and every moment. It allows me to enjoy the magic that is happening right now, especially when I go into nature or observe creatures. I begin to really appreciate my surroundings, the sanctity of life and the spontaneity of children as they live in the moment.

*"How to see the magic in everything and everywhere?*
*Slow down, that's how, and get out of your head.*
*The magic starts where thinking stops!"* (CL)

There is one other portal that is holy and affords me access to a deep connection with the divine; it is also one of the most fulfilling experiences that a human being can have, and that is because it allows my soul to be grateful, and to express its gratitude in a practical way. It is called Service. Most New Age people talk about Service in terms of fulfilling your soul's purpose in your current incarnation, e.g. being a healer, or a therapist, or performing some other selfless role that benefits others. As praiseworthy as that is, this is not the service that I am referring to; and that may not be the purpose to your life. Yes, it feels great to help our fellow brothers and sisters, to do good deeds, to be kind to others, and by all means let's please carry on doing that!

The service I have been fortunate enough to enjoy, is where the focus is on the divine will, having clarity about what needs to happen in order to manifest that, and thereby make something beautiful happen in this world; and acting to the best of my ability to make its progress as smooth as possible without getting in the way. This takes a high degree of consciousness on my part, and an openness or awareness of all the potential options that may or may not occur from one instant to the next. When I am engaged in a service opportunity with others as part of a team, there is a wonderful bond between us, a shared experience of something truly special. As one participant put it: "Service — there's no action like it!"

Service allows me to use my body and my intellect, to give of my time, and to be a part of something magical. It's like being a small but valuable cog in an intricate mechanism that gives meaning to the presence of the stars and to the rest of creation at this precise particular moment. On the surface, it looks as though I am giving, but actually I am receiving so much in terms of depth of experience and connection to the divine; I do it because I am grateful, but then I get filled up to overflowing again with the heart-felt connection to the divine lover ("the Beloved") and to the rewards of bliss that I feel are addressed to me personally. It's a degree of intimacy that meditation alone cannot reach. It is also the one area in my spiritual life where I experience the most Grace, being in the right place at the right time. Looking back on most of my experiences of service, I can see the synchronicity in what occurred. It's like being "on automatic pilot" and allowing God to move you on his chess board.

*"Do you have Space for Grace in your life?*
*Make room today for the divine to work through you*
*and good feelings will abound!"* (CL)

*"How to imbue your actions with the utmost quality?*
*Stay connected! Be conscious! Let EVERYTHING you do*
*come from Love. First Be, then Do..."* (CL)

As I write these words, without a traditional publishing deal, and with no real job security or any financial safety net, I can say to you that I have never felt happier. I am experiencing so much bliss, I feel really "happy in my own skin", and I also feel on the brink of an exciting adventure where I get to share my passion for Consciousness with more and more interested people. Because the experiences I have been talking about have deepened and expanded my spiritual awareness whilst writing about them and made them more consistent, I have become more inspired to share my authentic self and my truth on a daily basis with anyone and everyone.

In the past, I would have been careful to pick and choose my moments; and perhaps thirty years ago humanity hadn't yet sunk to the spiritually lacking abyss in which it now finds itself. We are so deeply entrenched in the quagmire of Unconsciousness that words of Truth are needed now more than ever! I'm doing my best to live a conscious life; will you join me?

*"We may be multi-dimensional beings with many past and future lives, however our Soul's only purpose is to be aware of our divinity NOW!"* (CL)

*"Yesterday, I was clever, so I wanted to change the world. Today, I am wise, so I am changing myself."* (Rumi)

*"Nature / Nurture? Our true nature is Divine Love. Make time every day to go within to nurture and manifest this in the world for everyone's sake!"* (CL)

*"Who or What you are is not a name, job title or relationship — it's a consciousness and a feeling. That feeling is Love. First Be, then Do."* (CL)

*"Is there anything greater than Love? It sustains all and needs to know itself! This is the reason and purpose behind your creation. Go within to discover the Universe of Love inside your heart."* (CL)

*"Be at peace within. If you cannot find it inside, you
certainly won't find it in this world."* (CL)

*"Is today going to be just a 'Doing' Day or a 'Being' Day?
Can you go about your business consciously,
i.e. aware of your divinity?"* (CL)

*"Every moment is a gift, the next breath God-given!
Consciousness of that truth leads to gratitude and bliss!"*
(CL)

*"We are billions of souls, all fragments of the One Soul
which is Spirit/God consciousness expressing itself. Expand
your awareness now and feel the love!"* (CL)

*"May I remind you? The way forward for you right now
requires no movement or action, rather it is a remembrance
of your true divine nature. First Be, then Do!"* (CL)

*"If no next breath means death, then each new breath
is a Rebirth and another opportunity to fulfil your life's
true purpose. Do ~ It ~ Now!"* (CL)

*"Why do we look outside for fulfilment — whether in the
form of Love, Peace, Truth or God? It's within,
always has been, always will be."* (CL)

*"Have no fear for every step in life is guided if you would but allow it to be so. Follow the deep and silent signals of the Heart."* (CL)

*"Looking for a miracle? Life is a miracle. You ARE the miracle!"* (CL)

*"The only way you can truly know Who you are (Soul) is by experiencing What you are (God/Spirit)!"* (CL)

*"Memo: Be kind to yourself today and wish that feeling for others when in their company — that is love. Pass it on!"* (CL)

*"Life is a gift, breaths are given not taken. How often today will you STOP just to admire the beauty and simplicity in every part of creation?"* (CL)

*"Inspiro: Latin for 'I breathe into'. For true inspiration, still body and mind, and focus on who or what is breathing you with so much love."* (CL)

*"Regular Heart Checks. It's good to regularly check in with your Heart to rediscover how beautiful you are! How about now?"* (CL)

*"Look outside at this planet... Go within...
The evidence is overwhelming! The creator's love is
everywhere and that Love loves you."* (CL)

*"The Light that illumines life's path is found inside.
Sometimes our next step is to STAY where we are and
to GROW in wisdom and self-knowledge."* (CL)

*"Do you know that everything is interconnected?
By universal love? That means that everything you say
or do to another you do to yourself..."* (CL)

*"In the History of the Universe, Creation and Evolution,
it all comes down to THIS perfect moment...
Is NOW perfect for you too?"* (CL)

*"Wonderful (Full of Wonder): Be Aware of the Oneness
in You, me, the flowers, creatures and all of creation,
and have a Oneder-full Day!"* (CL)

*"Spirituality is not about 'being nice' to one another.
It's about connecting inside to the experience that Spirit
and Love sustain all."* (CL)

*"Life is happening right now! Why wait for the intoxicating
fragrance of a flower, the sight of a gentle butterfly, or the
vastness of a clear and starlit sky to remind you that life is
good? Connect to that beautiful feeling inside now, all day!"*
(CL)

224

*"Every apparent worldly setback (and success!) is another opportunity for Surrender, to the love and grace within for true detachment and supreme perspective."* (CL)

*"'Namaste' means 'I greet your soul'. How often do you greet YOUR soul by bathing in your true form of divine Love and Light? Namaste!"* (CL)

*"In life we are told enjoying the journey is as important as reaching the destination. Each moment IS the destination!"* (CL)

*"We are truly blessed, yet most count their blessings in places that don't count."* (CL)

*"Desire is our greatest ally OR our greatest enemy. It will lead to fulfilment. The question is 'Whose? Our Mind's or our Heart's?'"* (CL)

*"I know I 'go on a bit' with my spiritual tweets, when really they all come down to one thing: Love loves you!"* (CL)

*"I wish for you a day filled with the miracles of the love and energy that we call Life, and an appreciation of your true divine nature."* (CL)

225

# CHAPTER FIVE

# *Is There Anybody Out There?*

## *(Do we have to do it all alone?)*

> *"What do you seek?"*
> *I said: "To have you as my constant friend."*
> *He said: "What do you want from me?"*
> *I said: "Your abundant grace."* (Rumi)

IN THE ABOVE QUOTE, who is Rumi talking to? He and virtually all the other mystic poets, some of whose heartfelt expressions have graced these pages, refer constantly to "the Beloved". Why does Rumi ask for abundant grace? Because he is already secure in the knowledge that he has his Beloved's love — there can be no doubt about this, it is felt strongly every time he turns his attention inside to connect to the source of that love. In feeling that love again, it deepens his own love for the beloved and gives rise to his soul's yearning for more of the same, and for that to always continue. Living in the world which demands our outside attention can easily make us forget that yearning — this is one good reason to ask for the beloved's abundant grace. I speak here from personal experience: once you are introduced to the divine, the path of your life transforms. It is then up to you to choose whether to go back, or to jump from one path to another, or to recognize which path's destination is the one you value.

Again, I ask: Who is "the Beloved"? Is he a romanticized figment of the imagination? Is he Jesus? Is he God?

If indeed there is a consciousness that has created all of matter (the universes, every life form, including souls inhabiting human bodies), and all of this has been done by and is sustained by Love, how inconceivable can it be — when human beings are seeking to fulfil the very purpose of their soul's existence and to merge with the Oneness, the Source, Spirit before death — that the Creator would not provide a guide, someone in the exact same human form as ourselves?

Traditionally, this guide ("guru" / "teacher" / "master" / "lord") is born like we are (the immaculate conception of Jesus being the exception), attains enlightenment at an early age, and becomes available to teach about the Supreme Consciousness. Once we gain greater understanding about our soul's purpose and are sufficiently thirsty for the experience of self-realization, of knowing our true self, he can, because of the divine grace that he has, connect us to the Truth, Love and Bliss inside ourselves which give us the Peace and true satisfaction our soul has been looking for.

There is always one of these divine incarnations existing on this planet whilst human beings are here at any one time; and to have more than one at any given time would create confusion. He may have students or disciples assisting him, but a seeker will find what he or she is looking for by asking for enlightenment or Knowledge of the self from the one and only embodiment at any given time. Jesus, the Christ (anointed one), was that embodiment two thousand years ago: *"I am the way, the truth and the life: no one comes to the Father, but by me"* he said (John 14:6). The direct experience of God that he revealed to the seekers of his time is available today. It

229

is *not* directly accessible through his teachings, or solely through a belief in him or God. All the scriptures are like sign posts, pointing you towards God's representative on Earth at the time. No offence implied, but the Pope is not this representative; a leader of Religion can never be, as religions only exist to celebrate past masters and their teachings, never the present-day living incarnation, even though they might make mention of the Second Coming! Even in the Buddhist traditions, the Buddha (enlightened one) is usually portrayed as portly, and yet images of Siddhartha Gautama himself show him as slim in build. Why is this? Did he gain weight once he attained nirvana? Of course not, the very traditional and more popular and acceptable representation of him, although historically inaccurate, is of the Buddha in his future incarnation.

Please, therefore, do not think for one second that you have to fulfil your spiritual journey all on your own, and without divine guidance! We may enter and depart this existence seemingly all alone, but there has always been a parallel path to our life's path, the path of Grace. And this is why Rumi also asks the Beloved to be his constant friend. Why? Because once he has revealed knowledge of our true self to us, the Beloved's external role is to remind us of our divinity, to drink regularly from the internal oasis of Peace when the world and our mind seek our constant attention. The relationship with the Beloved is two-way. When sat in his physical presence, I experience it as the caring love a father has for his child: so much care, so much love, so much kindness; but I also sense that, at the same time as I and everyone else in his presence are being reminded and inspired again and again, he too gains fulfilment and satisfaction from personal interaction and from sharing his guidance, wisdom and love. There have been many times in his presence that I have felt that "This truly is Heaven on Earth!" It is wonderful to be connected inside to the divine while sat in the company of the divine. Ironically, you cannot fully appreciate his divine presence until he has revealed the divine in you. Until that time, you may be watching and listening to him remotely via the internet, or even sitting not twenty metres from him while he is addressing you, but your mind will be racing with all its concepts of how this present-day incarnation/representative of God should dress, look, speak, act and be. Perhaps this is why Jesus, one of so many masters widely unrecognized in their time while alive, recommended that we approach him with the humility, openness and wonder of little children.

> *"I bow to you for the dust of your feet*
> *Is the crown on my head.*
> *And as I walk towards you*
> *Every step I take is a blessing."* (Rumi)

It isn't really until the Giver puts you in touch with the divine Source within you, and that you then begin to experience the creator's love behind every tangible aspect of this God experience, that the love flows and grows, and the respect you begin to have for the giver of the most holy then grows into love. *"Ye shall know them by their fruits"* Jesus said, remember? In this divine context the phrase "This could be the start of a beautiful relationship" turns into something of an understatement! As Rumi so aptly expresses it: *"It is Love and the Lover that live eternally — Don't lend your heart to anything else; all else is borrowed."*

*"You come to us from another world,*
*From beyond the stars and void of space.*
*Transcendent, pure, of unimaginable beauty.*
*Bringing with you the essence of Love.*
*You transform all who are touched by you.*
*Mundane concerns, trouble and sorrows*
*Dissolve in your presence,*
*Bringing joy to ruler and ruled, to peasant and king."*
(Rumi)

In the above expression Rumi describes so accurately the awe, love and respect my heart and soul feel when I am sat in the physical presence of the Beloved as he speaks, smiles and shines. There are many more mind-blowing things that I could say about the depth and personal nature of this special relationship with the Beloved, but they fall outside the remit of this guidebook. Suffice to say, there is (always) one special person on this planet that can show you God. Although I have accurately described the tangible attributes of the divine in Chapter

Three, the means of focusing on those aspects of God are ones that I came up with for the express purpose of allowing you to practise Meditation in that chapter. Firstly, I have no divine authority, grace or blessing that I can bestow on any other human being; I can only point, and sign-post, and wish you well. Secondly, not only does the Beloved Giver have the authority, and every grace and blessing that he is more than willing to bestow on any hungry heart, but he alone has the means of connecting you directly to the experience of self-knowledge and divine love which is waiting for you inside. He alone has the divine grace to do this, and he alone can provide you with the direct techniques (mine in Chapter Three are not as direct) to make it work for you. In any case, techniques without his Grace are "dry" and more like "hard work" in comparison, hence the unique significance of the Beloved. Grace makes it easier for us to *Be* divine rather than *Do* divine, especially when meditating.

Is it possible to experience one's divinity without an intermediary? Yes, I believe it is. I believe there are human beings who have done so, who do so today, and who will. At this point, I would like to express my gratitude and deepest appreciation to Eckhart Tolle. If I had not chanced upon "The Power Of Now" and found myself inspired by Eckhart's spiritual insights and the way he expressed his own experience of the human-divine relationship and the nature of the Universe and our place in it, I would not have been moved to express my own truth in **Human Being** ("Thank You" dear brother Eckhart). For whatever reason, and by whatever events in their life, there are souls who are blessed with a deep and meaningful connection to God's love inside themselves. It may have come at times of extreme peril or selflessness. And whether this is subsequently reliant on belief, or faith, or worship, I don't know. Surely Knowing, in comparison to Belief, etc., because you have experienced its tangible aspects and felt its love, makes it accessible and undeniable forever. Once you know, belief becomes redundant.

More importantly perhaps, to miss out on an opportunity to share a relationship with the Beloved both internally and externally when you are both in human form, is something I cannot adequately express to you, but with the following words I try in this *Expression to my Beloved*.

### The Greatest Miracle

*I am alive!*
*I have a body, a human body.*

*You told me the greatest miracle was each God-given breath.*
*I beg to differ.*

*I am here, and you are here.*
*That I am here, and that I can see you, listen to you,*
*Fill my heart from the bottomless well of your grace and mercy,*
*And join in the Line of Hearts that recognize your true form,*

*Your majesty, and divinity,*
*Is, for me, the greatest miracle.*

*I am the most fortunate, the truly blessed,*
*Only because of you!*

*I thank you with each and every God-given breath.*
*Thank you! Thank you! Thank you!*

Having the Beloved here while you are here means that whenever you need re-inspiring to maintain your level of consciousness or spiritual practice, not only can you read printed excerpts from his presentations and events, or watch recordings, but you can sit in his divine presence and hear it directly from him, heart to heart. Whenever I have taken this opportunity of physical proximity, even at the back of a huge hall, the intimacy he creates with his presence, love and care as he speaks, makes me feel that I am sat in his living room and that he is talking only to me, heart to heart, his to mine. By the way, for a supposed "holy man", this present-day Beloved has a wicked sense of humour! I don't think I have ever sat at any talk he has given without laughing many times. Leaving his presence, I once again have renewed clarity and focus, and am bursting with divine love. My body, mind, soul and life feel so much lighter, and my heart is overflowing again, although it may be tinged with the sadness of missing the physical presence of its Beloved already.

*"Joy is peace dancing. Peace is joy at rest."*
(Frederick Brotherton Meyer, English Evangelist)

Now please sincerely ask yourself: Are you at the point in your life where you are willing to stop being a professional seeker and are now ready to forgo the accumulation of intellectual knowledge in favour of the actual real and tangible experience of your true self, the divine consciousness behind your eyes and mind? If "Yes!", then please check out the Resources chapter. You will be able to make the connections that will take you to the fulfilment of your soul's purpose, its creation, and the reason behind your very existence.

*"Think of Life like this: it is your opportunity to
spend time with the best friend you ever had.
It is your chance to be with the ultimate clarity,
the ultimate kindness, the ultimate joy.
That's what a life is.
It's not promised to be forever, but the possibility exists that
you get to spend time with that which is the most beautiful.
And that resides in your heart."* (Prem Rawat,
spiritual teacher)

Remember my quote *"May I remind you? The way forward for you right now requires no movement or action, rather it is a remembrance of your true divine nature. First Be, then Do!"*? Until your true divine nature is revealed to you, until you discover what you really are, then how can you start to Be? To borrow from Shakespeare, and in a different context to Hamlet's dilemma: *"To be or not to be, that (really) is the question!"*

And now to conclude...

This is where the author, in his alias as the Self-Esteem Doctor, brings together the themes of Part One **Human Doing** and Part Two **Human Being**. I do this by borrowing from my Higher Self's quote *"Is there anything greater than Love? It sustains all and needs to know itself! This is the reason and purpose behind your creation. Go within to discover the Universe of Love inside your heart."*

Is there anything greater than Love? All the therapy and self-development processes in **Human Doing**, designed to elevate your self-esteem to optimum levels, are based on one simple premise. It's the same premise that was made apparent to me many years ago, and that led to the formation of my *It's Never too Late to Have a Happy Childhood!* inner child therapy process which I have taught around the world. And it is this: Love, when manifestly evident in one's life, via hugs, kisses and cuddles from family members, gives a soul security; this in turn naturally translates as good self-esteem and a healthy sense of self-worth in one's dealings with others and the world. Feeling and knowing that you are loved are essential ingredients to a happy life.

And now, moving to the more spiritual aspect of **Human Being**, can you imagine what it would be like to have the most tangible experience of the Greatest

Love? Being loved inside by the creator of your soul, and feeling and *knowing* without any doubt who you are, what you are! This is the ultimate security, and the ultimate self-esteem! As the Self-Esteem Doctor, can I give you that? No, but "I know a man who can!"

May you receive more blessings in your life than you have already, and may your next steps lead to the realization of your life's true purpose and to the fulfilment of your birthright. Peace, and bliss-full wishes, from my heart to yours!

> *"The only thing that remains real is the Heart.*
> *Untouched by human beings ever since Time.*
> *And that is where the Truth exists.*
> *Truth — the Truth.*
> *The only place where it is pure.*
> *And the only place where the real Love resides.*
> *And that is the place where the master comes to take you to,*
> *And the magic happens again and again and again*
> *On the face of this Earth."* (Prem Rawat)

# CHAPTER SIX

# *Resources*

*www.wopg.org*

Printed in Great Britain
by Amazon

65373763R00156